55

ANCIENT ⊞ modern

ANCIENT
+modern

Cynthia Inions

Photography by Simon Upton

Jacqui
Small

Publisher: Jacqui Small
Project editor: Stuart Cooper
Copy editor: Tessa Clark
Designer: Lawrence Morton
Stylist: Cynthia Inions
Production: Geoff Barlow

First published in 2001
by Jacqui Small,
an imprint of Aurum Press Ltd,
25 Bedford Avenue,
London WC1B 3AT

A catalogue record for this book is
available from the British Library.

ISBN 1 903221 05 6

Printed in Hong Kong

CONTENTS

Introduction 6

Concept 10

Structure 34

Function 74

Elements 104

Details 128

Resources 156

Index 158

Acknowledgements 160

In the downtown New York studio of sculptor Elena Colombo, special attention is given to the importance of colour, shape, light and presentation. Placing a simple modern glass jar on top of an old dark wooden chest in front of a pale blue-painted brick wall creates a compelling composition.

INTRODUCTION

Combining ancient and modern — from adding a twenty-first-century extension to a nineteenth-century town house to standing a modern oak table on an ancient kilim or fitting a stainless-steel sink in a sixteenth-century farmhouse kitchen — is an exciting and practical way to create a contemporary home.

A+m

Combining ancient and modern is not new. Throughout history, whether through inheritance or acquisition, people have adapted existing buildings and incorporated furniture and objects from previous generations and different cultures to create comfortable, individual – and at times fashionable – homes. At the beginning of the nineteenth century simple and economic rural Scandinavian style embraced the influences of French decorative rococo and neoclassicism to create an original – and in time influential – look of its own. These additions did not displace what existed, partly because so much furniture was ingeniously built in to the simple wooden structures in which people lived, to optimize space. Swedish Gustavian style was characterized by signature combinations of the decorative and the plain, the grand and the simple, with natural textures, plain walls and simple colours alongside checked or striped fabrics in red, blue or yellow and white, gilded or decorative detailing and painted wooden furniture.

Equally, there are historic precedents to the way many people choose to live now. Open-plan integrated interiors were common in medieval times; the ancient Romans preferred low-level relaxation on large floor cushions; and a modern Eames chaise longue is reminiscent of a Victorian one or even an ancient African daybed.

What is different about combining ancient and modern today, however, is a general freedom and confidence in our own sense of style, and a range of architectural opportunities to create original and individual living spaces. In the last ten years the availability of an ever-increasing range of non-domestic spaces to convert into dwellings, and our access through media exposure to the work of imaginative and influential architects and designers, has had a massive impact on our perception of a contemporary home.

At the beginning of the twenty-first century combining ancient and modern has also become important from an ecological point of view, as regenerating and reinventing existing buildings helps to preserve precious resources. Examples include the conversion of former industrial buildings into domestic dwellings, as in contemporary loft developments, and the restoration and

modernization of historic homes, as in the revival of Victorian-Gothic wooden housing in San Francisco's Bay area.

An ancient and modern aesthetic can be applied both in terms of architecture and in the creation of interiors. Adding dynamic contemporary extensions and architectural features to existing buildings; paring down historic homes to create simpler spaces; or combining antique and modern furniture, textiles, art and artefacts in bold juxtapositions – these are all ways of creating individual and enjoyable spaces to live in. Ancient and modern can be combined in the very structure of a home or in simple details, such as using antique teacups with a contemporary teapot when you serve tea.

The aim of this book is to present these different options by showing, describing and celebrating a diverse range of inspiring interiors and ideas, all of which demonstrate the exciting new opportunities there are today for exploring ancient and modern combinations. Indeed, of the many homes featured, only three existed in anything like their present form ten years ago; most of the interiors photographed and described have been created much more recently. Five years ago two former industrial buildings were either derelict or in the process of being restored and converted. One living and working space was a professional design studio; another was an office. A nineteenth-century house has been totally reorganized since the arrival of children. And an apartment in Paris has been transformed by replacing antique furniture with modern iconic designs. These spaces are now exciting ancient and modern environments, which acknowledge the architecture and function of the original buildings and provide contemporary homes that meet the different requirements of those who live in them.

Combining ancient and modern is a way of expressing our individual style. Where we live and the buildings we live in, how we organize and decorate our homes, and the furniture, textiles, art and artefacts we surround ourselves with tell our stories. The material used for a floor, the colour of a wall, the shape of a pot or the patina of a table – all reveal our interests, passions and cultural influences, and all add soul and texture to our homes.

OPPOSITE Traditional Japanese style is contrasted with bold contemporary architecture in this loft-style apartment in London. The wall has a textured render and the floor tiles are authentic riven slate. The space provides a dynamic backdrop to oriental antiques and artefacts.

CONCEPT

'To be modern is not a fashion, it is a state. It is necessary to understand history, and he who understands history knows how to find continuity between that which was, that which is, and that which will be.' Le Corbusier

Putting together diverse ancient and modern elements, whether it is a contemporary metal table with nineteenth-century cutlery or an ancient Indian daybed on a white felt rug, brings out what is special and strong about them.

Any environment provides opportunities for combining ancient and modern, both in the structure of a building and the relationship between the structure and the elements within it. An attic apartment in Paris, for example, has nineteenth-century oak beams, wrought-iron window balustrades and modern European furniture; the loft conversion of a former garment factory in New York combines matt concrete floors, white walls and oriental antiques; and a conventional Victorian town house in London has a two-level glass extension at its rear.

Living in a space that combines ancient and modern is about coexistence and balance. Coexistence essentially means acknowledging our architectural heritage and finding ways to change or direct it into the kinds of spaces we want to live in. Balance is about incorporating compelling details from the past – whether these are the architectural features of a building or pieces of furniture, textiles, art or artefacts – with our present and future requirements for our homes.

This chapter explains the terms 'ancient' and 'modern' in relation to creating a contemporary space and describes how the two concepts can be harnessed to create a powerful and enriching design aesthetic. It examines the wide range of choices we have when it comes to selecting a place to live and the different perspectives or starting points from which old and new might be brought together. It also outlines the key principles for combining ancient and modern – either to create striking juxtapositions that throw structures, elements or objects into sharp relief, or to explore the connections between shapes and forms from widely different centuries and cultures.

Finally, the chapter introduces a theme that is central to the book: how an ancient and modern aesthetic enables us to create individual homes that reflect our diverse tastes and influences and tell our personal stories.

Contexts

The coexistence and balance of ancient and modern is an important theme in our cultural and day-to-day lives. Ancient forms and concepts are apparent in architecture, design and fashion, from a dome or arch to a pair of denim jeans. Such forms appear as recurring templates – for example, the shapes and lack of ornamentation of nineteenth-century cutlery is evident in the modern design classics of David Mellor. Or they can inspire reinvention, for instance a *stella* or Roman magistrate's stool was the inspiration for Mies van der Rohe's Barcelona chair, first produced in 1929.

An ancient and modern dynamic has been used in high-profile public buildings like the Tate Modern in London and the Louvre in Paris. For the Tate Modern, which opened at the beginning of the new millennium, architects Jacques Herzog and Pierre de Meuron reinvented a partly redundant industrial building to create a space for exhibiting large-scale installations. The voluminous turbine hall of the original structure has been laid bare and acts as host to a series of interconnecting galleries. In Paris the startling glass pyramid rising bang in the centre of the Louvre is a symbol of creative bravado by architect Ieoh Ming Pei. The transparent structure, with fountains and three smaller pyramids in its court, underlines the symmetry of the former thirteenth-century palace.

In furniture design the purity and practicality of eighteenth- and nineteenth-century Shaker furniture is visible in many contemporary chairs, tables and storage units. A 4-metre-long table made for a workshop in Cambridge, Massachusetts, is a typical example of ancient Shaker furniture, with a simple construction, tapering legs, and wheels to facilitate movement and cleaning. Similar simple worktables with wheels are today sold by retailers such as IKEA for use in contemporary flexible living spaces.

In Japan, following the revolutionary deconstruction fashion of Rei Kawakubo of Comme Des Garcons, the fabric technology of Issey Miyake and the inventive tailoring of Yohji Yamamoto, designs from a new generation that is looking to reconnect with ancient traditions include contemporary T-shirts with pockets made from fragments of antique silk kimonos.

All these cultural developments are inspiring examples of how old and new can be interpreted and combined. They demonstrate the strength and relevance of an ancient and modern aesthetic as a response to the big issues of the twenty-first century: finding a continuum between what exists and the future; making the best possible use of available and valuable resources; and – possibly the biggest issue of all – creating aesthetically and culturally rich environments.

RIGHT Slate tiles with a riven or uneven surface provide authentic Japanese flooring in an oriental-inspired loft. Simple utility pieces like this antique footstool contrast with strident architecture to create a powerful ancient and modern environment.
OPPOSITE Contemporary details and fittings, such as industrial steel windows and fin radiators, provide a high-specification setting for oriental furniture. The apartment, like Tate Modern seen through the window, is representative of the regeneration of former industrial buildings into vital contemporary spaces.

THIS PAGE In an imaginative conversion of a brick factory in New Jersey, an ancient hand-hewn African bed is juxtaposed with contemporary cost-efficient plywood flooring, which in turn contrasts with the nineteenth-century architecture.
OPPOSITE A mid-twentieth-century chair by Jean Prouvé, with an oak frame and a birch-veneered plywood seat and back, combines traditional carpentry with machine technology.

Defining ancient and modern

Exploring definitions of ancient and modern is an important part of our understanding and enjoyment of an ancient and modern aesthetic. This is not an academic endeavour; the aim of this book is to provide inspiration and ideas for combining two vital forces in contemporary culture. And while identifying examples of what is ancient and what is modern is a good way to acknowledge the differences between objects made centuries apart, it is thrilling also to discover similarities. A Georgian three-prong fork and an eighteenth-century Japanese footstool share a simplicity and practicality that makes them every bit as relevant and welcome in a contemporary space as a twenty-first-century chair by Marc Newson.

In the context of this book, 'ancient' refers to buildings, furniture and objects made before industrial machinery and production. A house with a basic frame made from

wooden joists and brick pillars – not steel and concrete – is an example. And although industrial manufacturing and mass-production techniques have largely replaced the making of building materials and furniture by hand, our heritage of expert craftsmanship and classic design is still a vital part of contemporary life. The structures that provide homes for many people, a competitive trade in every kind of antique from before the machine age – from architectural salvage to glassware – and a general passion for flea markets, second-hand shops and grandparents' attics all bear testament to this.

The trace of humanity in the way ancient artefacts were made is an essential factor in their enduring popularity, but their patina of wear and use is equally central to their appeal in a contemporary home. An Early American cupboard with peeling paint, an eroded stone step or weather-beaten brick wall in a Victorian schoolhouse conversion, the darkened wood on the arms of a chair or the random crisscrossing of marks on a copper bath – such traces of the past are visual and textural reminders of a previous existence and add layers of meaning and mystery to any surface. And perhaps we are also drawn to these handmade things, with their imperfections and the resonance and secrets they hold, because there is only a finite number of ancient buildings, pieces of furniture, art and artefacts.

Whereas 'ancient' can be defined relatively easily, 'modern' is both a design direction and a perspective or way of seeing. In many ways, to be modern is to be of the moment yet forward-looking. Yet, as this book illustrates, being modern can mean looking to the past as well as to the future. At the start of the twentieth century, however, 'modern' was a clear-cut concept: it was a rejection of everything from previous centuries – styles like rococo, Gothic and Empire. The beginning of the machine age, mass production and the introduction of materials like tubular steel, bent plywood and aluminium provide a logical division between ancient and modern architecture and design. In design terms the machine age began around 1910, and within twenty years the concept of a contemporary home had changed significantly. For example, by the 1930s and 1940s appliances and consumer goods such as refrigerators and vacuum cleaners were commonplace throughout the USA and western Europe.

Yet this was not a period of single-minded progression in architecture and design. People like Le Corbusier, Alvar Aalto, Eileen Gray, Charlotte Perriand and Jean Prouvé were producing diverse and inspiring work, developing signature styles and gaining a following

amongst modern-thinking consumers. Meanwhile, however, the mass market remained fixed on traditional concepts and interiors.

During the twentieth century, design progressed from the radical visions of the Modernist Movement in the 1930s to the domestic retail revolution of Habitat with its colourful dispensable sofas in the 1960s and, finally, to the minimalist contemporary homes created at the end of the century. All were very different – and all were 'modern'. Designers and architects including Charles Eames, Frank Gehry, Arne Jacobsen, Mies van der Rohe and Frank Lloyd Wright, and minimalist architects like Tadao Ando, Luis Barragán and John Pawson, have set new standards and principles in modern design. And, like the duvet generation of the 1970s who gave up traditional bedlinen overnight in universal favour of big lightweight sacks of feathers, once the concepts and ideas of these designers and architects were out in the open they were assimilated for everyday use.

And while technology may have transformed our living spaces in many ways – from the low-maintenance, eco-friendly materials used to build contemporary homes, to shopping on the Internet, watering our gardens by remote control, deflating plastic chairs to fit our body shape and programming a lighting system to dim gradually while we eat supper – a modern lifestyle is not complex or inaccessible. A home that is essentially of the twenty-first century is instantly recognizable because of its informality, diversity and freedom. It is possible to be modern yet live in a nineteenth-century house with no central heating and few electric lights, or in a contemporary loft with second-hand sofas and junk-shop tables and chairs. Just as it is possible to be modern and live in a former brick factory with an eclectic mix of American and European twentieth-century furniture, or in a reinvention of an Edwardian house with antiques from Rajasthan and industrial metal stairs. Individual and enjoyable combinations of furniture, objects, colours and textures, and a general sense of light and simplicity, all contribute to the atmosphere of a modern space.

Being modern is about putting together different elements with regard to shape, form and meaning and without regard to age, style or origin. Seeing apparent similarities, for example in shape, form and colour, makes us look longer to seek out the differences, and this ultimately deepens our appreciation of ancient and modern. This book sets out to bring together inspiring examples of ancient and modern combinations – not as answers or formulas but as a celebration of individual stories and interpretations.

An ancient and modern aesthetic

An ancient and modern aesthetic influences the way a space looks and how it feels to live in. It is a way of evaluating and responding to a structure, a chair or a door handle – whether these are ancient or modern – and will inform and direct your overall design concept for a building or room. An ancient and modern aesthetic can translate into an historic space with a capsule collection of iconic twentieth-century furniture, or a contemporary home with second-hand furniture found in junk shops or skips. In either case, what you choose to leave out is just as important as the pieces you include.

However, creating an ancient and modern space is not about insensitively removing or obsessively obliterating architectural details in an effort to optimize light and openness, leaving only the bare structure itself to represent ancient. The essence of a place is in the architraving and door hinges as much as it is in large-scale structural elements like its facade. Although there may be a good reason for simplifying an interior by keeping only the minimum of original features – for example you may want to reduce excessive decorative details or remove the walls to create an open-plan family area – it is important to be selective in what you take away and what you keep.

Nor is an ancient and modern aesthetic about preserving details simply because they are there, or totally restoring a building. Where is the vitality or energy in a space that does not change? Contemporary homes that work for the people who live in them evolve in response to changes in circumstances and new perspectives on lifestyle.

Architectural features are only one factor in an overall space. Furniture, textiles, lighting, art and artefacts are equally essential, and add an enlivening multilayering of shape, colour, form and historic or cultural references. However, it is important to use these elements selectively so that they coexist with, and balance, each other and their architectural surroundings. Creating clear and simple combinations of ancient and modern within a space, or in relation to the structure of a space, draws attention to the individual elements and to what connects them or makes them different.

Ancient and modern perspectives

Developing a space with an ancient and modern aesthetic means acknowledging the scale and style of the original structure, considering its merits and potential, and creating a design that is sympathetic to the existing architecture and appropriate to individual requirements. This is true of any project, whether it involves converting a barn into a living/working space for an urban couple, designing a contemporary home for a family with a collection of antiques or simplifying an interior as a backdrop to an eclectic mix of furniture and artefacts.

A direct way of implementing an ancient and modern aesthetic is to add or incorporate the opposite of what exists already – for example, to extend an ancient structure with a modern one, to refit a raw industrial space with slick, high-specification materials or to introduce modern furniture into an historic house. This will create a powerful juxtaposition between different structures or between the structure of a building and the elements within it. However, a less direct response can provide opportunities for effective connections between existing and new structures and elements. For example, in a cowshed conversion in Cornwall the existing ancient building was extended with an identical structure, and the whole was furnished with a collection of contemporary and antique furniture and art.

In architect John Pawson's conversion of a traditional timber-frame barn in England a few essential items of furniture offset the vast canopy of oak beams in the main living space. Every wall is painted white and he has introduced new elements, such as a concrete floor throughout a series of interconnecting spaces, that are in keeping with the natural qualities of the structure. Pawson's reinvention focuses on an exhilarating sense of openness and creates an extraordinary contemporary environment.

In London, architect Pip Horne's custom-built house for the artist Anish Kapoor is a very different project. The structure is all new, with sculptural white walls spiralling through a central atrium, yet the artist's collection of heritage Indian icons and an eclectic mix of colourful and decorative antiquities transform the experience of being in the house. This is as powerful an example of an ancient and modern aesthetic as Pawson's barn, but is different in almost every aspect.

In a New York loft an inexpensive way of transforming the structure of a space provides the key to a dynamic combination of ancient and modern. In fashion designer Han Feng's conversion of a former factory everything is the same colour. This simplifies and unifies a network of pipes and girders and provides a plain backdrop to oriental antiques, muslin banners and brightly coloured silk lanterns. This contrast between the structure of a space and the elements within it can be applied to many different settings.

The key principle of an ancient and modern aesthetic is to respond to the original structure and retain a sense of place. In Gert van de Keuken's Art Deco apartment in Paris the structure has been laid bare with white walls and beige-painted concrete floors. This reduces a dominant architectural style to a simple backdrop with a sense of proportion and light. Classic twentieth-century furniture and junk-shop tables and chairs combine to create a welcoming and texturally rich space.

Architect Pierre d'Avoine's extension of a suburban London house centres on views and access to the garden. New openings in the existing structure and sliding glass doors at the back create long views through the house and a light, spacious living area.

Juxtaposition and connection

Different combinations of ancient and modern are based on the principles of juxtaposition and connection, and they radically alter and influence the way a space and everything within it is perceived. These principles can be applied whether you are arranging a cup and plate, putting together a capsule collection of furniture or exposing an original architectural feature in a building. Simple juxtapositions and connections of colour, texture and shape have a significant impact. Yet it is equally valid and workable to create historic and cultural combinations or your own esoteric theme.

Essentially, juxtaposition is a way of directing attention to differences between the structure and the elements in a space, or between the elements themselves. An example is the dining area in a conversion of a former nineteenth-century church in Yorkshire, which is furnished with a handmade wooden table and machine-made white Arne Jacobsen chairs. Connection is about finding and underlining links and common themes. For example, black-and-white photographic portraits from the Edwardian era could be displayed in plain white box frames.

Juxtaposition is a powerful dynamic. It is often through this that the true nature of a thing, whether it is a building or a fork, becomes apparent. Placing a round white bowl next to a rectangular black vase brings the different colour and shape of each vessel into focus. Putting a round white bowl against a concrete wall or a block of colour brings out, and draws attention to, individual surfaces and forms; it changes the way we see and experience both the bowl and the wall. Black and white, round and angular are bold and direct juxtapositions. Equally direct are textural contrasts – of rough and smooth, for example the natural surface of a bamboo table and the industrial polish of a stainless-steel bowl; or matt and glossy – flat-glazed walls and gloss-painted floors.

Presenting ancient or ethnic items in a contemporary setting isolates them from their usual cultural references and gives them impact and definition. For example, an African tribal doll in a pared-down Art Deco apartment, or an antique French chair with a gold frame and linen seat on a black-and-white vinyl floor, are seen in a completely new way.

Ancient and modern juxtapositions translate effectively into architecture, furniture, art, artefacts and everyday utilitarian fittings and equipment. Place a mid-twentieth-century standard lamp alongside a Gothic stone fireplace set flat into a plain plaster wall and the composition will project a visual sparkle that is profoundly different to the impact of the lamp or fireplace in isolation. Insert an industrial-style staircase in a conventional Edwardian house, or add a grandmother's collection of wooden spoons to a battery of stainless-steel kitchen utensils, and time

RIGHT This black-and-white combination is a dynamic juxtaposition of historic architecture and contemporary furniture design in the form of a 1950s Arne Jacobsen chair. The split wood of the walls and floors also makes a visual connection with the worn and cracked leather on the chair.

A+M

after time the power of these ancient and modern juxtapositions will strengthen and underline the shape, form and meaning of the individual elements.

In structural terms there are many opportunities for juxtaposing ancient and modern. In an historic house simply uncovering original floorboards to reveal a rich patina of wear will provide a textural contrast to anything with a machine edge – contemporary metal furniture, perhaps, or a concrete platform or steps. In industrial conversions the function and design of the original building is an alien context for contemporary furniture and fittings. It is this that provides the opportunities for juxtaposition, and many conversions retain essential and authentic architectural details. Unfortunately, if key original features like metal windows or shutters have been removed it is impossible to replace them.

Connection is an alternative way of combining elements in a space. It is used to create visual and textural harmony, for example by grouping different kinds of chairs that are all made of beechwood or that originate in the 1950s. Beginning with two or three pieces, perhaps a dining table and chairs, which have a simple connection that works well in a space is a good way to develop a capsule collection of furniture. In illustrator Max Gustafson's New York loft most of the furniture comes from trips to neighbourhood flea markets. Pale grey and blue rustic wooden cupboards, all in a similar state of distress and wear, bare wooden tables and chairs and basic country-style pottery combine harmoniously to add texture and natural shapes to an industrial environment. Creating a connection like this between different elements links them visually and groups them within an overall scheme so that no single piece dominates an environment.

Introducing colour – either a single hue or a family of colours – is an effective way to create a sense of unity and simplicity. If you decide to use just one colour, for example on walls, floors and furniture, add texture and variation with different finishes. In an all-white scheme a mix of gloss and matt paints and peeling patinas adds sensory and visual stimulation to a simple interior.

A family or palette of colours, whether they are based on historic colours found in original Shaker houses or are akin to those in Andy Warhol's Pop Art paintings, can be used to define different groups of elements while maintaining an overall harmony. For example, in a pared-down historic house a palette of earthy browns connects 1930s leather sofas, European rustic tables, funky 1970s high-back

chairs in suede and ethnic wooden bowls from Africa. All these pieces are set against bare floorboards and white walls on all four levels – a simple structural space.

Look for compatibility and connections between shapes and forms. In the open-plan, pared-down Paris apartment of French interior designer Frederic Mechiche imaginative connections are made between similar shapes and forms in ancient African artefacts, for example a tribal mask, and contemporary art photography, such as a modern portrait, set against a backdrop of antique white panelling and pale, bare floorboards. In Alastair Gordon and Barbara de Vries' converted brick factory in New Jersey a French daybed in worn leather with a ticking mattress connects with an ancient African

bed made from a single piece of wood. Both items of furniture occupy centrepiece positions within different areas. The French daybed is on the ground floor and the African bed is on the mezzanine level. And while it is difficult to see both pieces at the same time, one clearly echoes the other and the connection between them crosses centuries and cultures.

To make effective connections using functional items such as fixtures and fittings, it is best to focus on simple combinations like a Victorian roll-top bath with second-hand taps in a contemporary bathroom, or a stainless-steel sink and laboratory taps in an ancient kitchen. On a smaller scale the pleasure of using a collection of ancient and modern storage jars or ceramic tableware, and the

texture and patina that they bring to a contemporary home, will override any mismatching of historic detail or style.

To create connections between structural elements, such as floors, windows and doors, take your lead from existing original features. Connections between materials work well, for example installing new flat-panel oak doors in keeping with original oak parquet flooring, or laying a concrete floor next to an original stone floor. Be careful when using architectural salvage from a very different environment to yours: antique doors from India require a lot of plain space to look good. Also, installing a wide variety of elements out of their original context can lead to a jumble of references that will distract from the sense of connection.

RIGHT With its plain, functional design this Georgian glass is remote from changing styles. Its classic outline and fine form set the standard for contemporary glassware. OPPOSITE The parallels in simplicity and construction between this antique wooden country-style table and contemporary metal chair connect across centuries.

Ancient and modern motifs

The shape and form of many contemporary products, usually workaday tools like spoons, cooking pots, baskets and bath taps, have not changed over centuries. Although in some cases the way they are manufactured has altered beyond recognition – spoons that were once made individually by hand are now mass-produced by machines – their basic form, or template, remains the same. Equally, many current handmade products and crafts, for example a bent-plank stool or a ceramic bowl, are versions of ancient templates. This is most clearly seen in traditional products and designs. For example, in architects Ushida Findlay's loft conversion in London's Bankside development handmade Japanese shoji screens in wood and paper provide lightweight space dividers without blocking light or reducing the structure's flexibility and sense of openness – precisely how shoji screens have always been used.

Successfully combining ancient functional or utility items, for exampl such as china plates and teapots, depends upon choosin

This African workstool succeeds on a functional as well as an aesthetic level. It is lightweight and portable, and encourages the sitter to keep a straight back with feet on the ground and weight evenly distributed. With its simplicity and graphic outline it is ancient and yet modern.

The simple poetry and precision of this clay teapot with a bamboo handle was created by refining and simplifying a basic design through generations. Its smooth surface and organic form make it perfect for holding in both hands. When the pot is in use, the clay keeps the tea hot, and the bamboo handle stays cool for carrying and pouring.

The visual appearance of a table knife – its colour, patina and shape – is a vital part of its appeal in a contemporary home. Yet it is also important to consider how it feels to use – its weight and balance in the hand, the smoothness and length of the handle, and the sharpness of the blade. These plain utilitarian knives work well in an eclectic table setting.

**ntique glassware and cutlery, with everyday contemporary items,
imple, undecorated shapes and forms.**

This hand-beaten metal cross is ancient African money. The size of an adult's hand and the weight of a small chicken, it is as much a powerful symbol of wealth as a practical means of exchanging or transferring it. The cross is also remarkably modern and sculptural in its form.

The utilitarian style of this spoon originated in the nineteenth century – a combination of the traditional skills of English silversmiths and the flamboyant style of Huguenot artisans. The advent of industrial production and a general climate for setting design standards in everything from buildings to tablespoons made it possible to buy multiples of this simple design.

Inexpensive ethnic cooking utensils, like this oriental ladle and African wooden spoon, provide a hands-on connection with ancient traditional crafts and resourceful low-tech design. The joint between the scoop and handle expands to a tight fit when the utensil is in use.

A personal space

Few people are content to inherit a previous occupant's interpretation of a space, let alone ideas and configurations from fifty years ago. We all seek to reinvent what we inherit or where we live. An ancient and modern aesthetic is a way of incorporating history and heritage in a contemporary environment without being nostalgic. It offers an opportunity to make the best use of existing options and strengthens our ability to conceptualize alternatives.

By liberating us from conventional values that place greater importance on things we know to be expensive antiques or good investments, an ancient and modern aesthetic enables us to celebrate architectural features and other elements in a space for their own sake. A flea-market plate can contribute as much visual delight to a table setting as an antique candelabra. In the same way it is possible to orientate a sitting room around a simple window with a pleasant view rather than an historically important Gothic marble fireplace, or to stand a contemporary painting in front of the fireplace to take it out of the space altogether.

Family treasures, hand-me-downs and objects of personal significance can be included in a space without compromising the overall scheme or the objects themselves. Alternatively, such items can be presented or contained in a way that is in keeping with a specific style. For example, an antique wooden cupboard can be integrated into a contemporary white apartment by painting a wall or section of wall a mellow grey to support the piece of furniture and reduce any conflict between the elements.

It is in our nature to avoid exclusivity and look to many different sources for emotional, aesthetic – and even spiritual – stimulation and fulfilment. Therefore it is logical and appropriate to bring together disparate elements or objects to create an inspirational and enjoyable place to live. For example, a New York loft conversion belonging to an English and American couple has a mix of European antique furniture, contemporary American art and ethnic textiles from India, Morocco and Turkey. An ancient and modern aesthetic is a positive approach to creating a home that is a true reflection of our individual style.

While it is good to plan and consider options, it is best to avoid being obsessive or over-academic about specific historic details or design icons. Trust yourself and your instincts about how you want to live. It is often the accidental or expedient decision – perhaps choosing to do something because it is quick and inexpensive rather than the best way of furthering a grand scheme – that enhances a space beyond expectation.

In isolation the elements and objects in this New York loft, which include a flea-market lampstand and china, a table made out of new wood, and aluminium chairs, would appear low-key and commonplace. However, bringing them together creates an individual and engaging ancient and modern space.

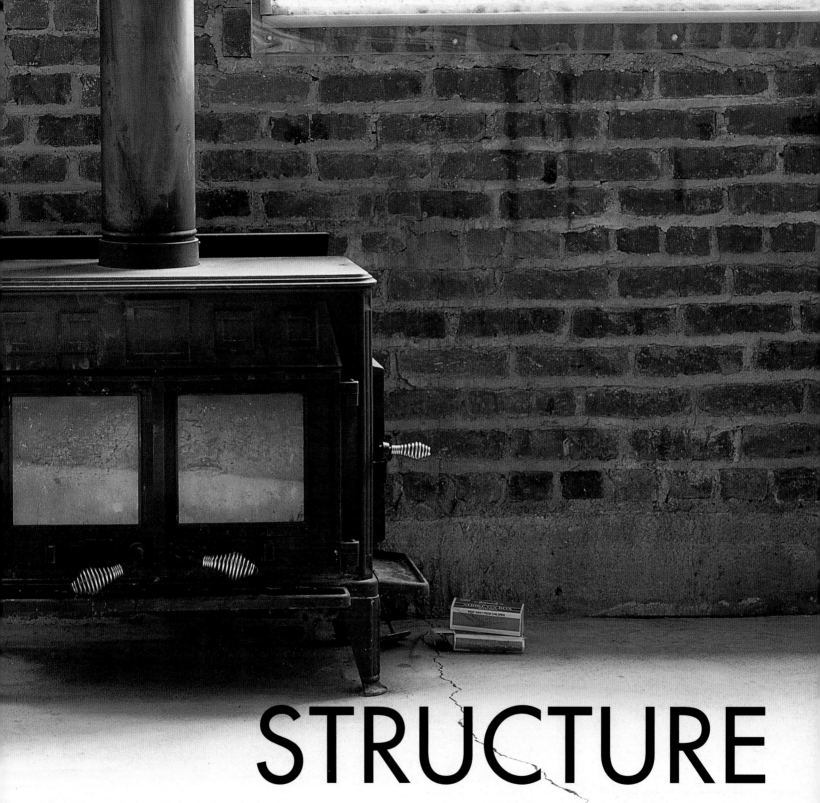

STRUCTURE

'A good space
will accommodate
an Empire chair
every bit as well as
a Corbusier chaise.'
Doris Saatchi

THIS PAGE
The structure of this
open-plan New York
studio is new, apart
from the antique
Moroccan doors
leading to a bedroom.
Recently built on top
of an existing block,
the space is a double-
height construction
with glass walls at
either end.
PREVIOUS PAGES
The ancient and
modern architectural
solution for this
converted brick
factory in New Jersey
included exposing the
structure of the space
and using materials
such as concrete, raw
wood and steel.

Altering an existing structure in any way, from remodelling the internal architecture to simply repainting it, offers many opportunities to reinvent your home, add to the enjoyment of living in a space and combine ancient and modern.

From large-scale projects such as dismantling and reworking the interior of a conventional town house or converting a former factory to an open-plan loft space, to smaller projects like refurbishing a rural shack or simply exposing and repairing an original floor, there are many imaginative and resourceful ideas to inspire and encourage us to undertake structural projects of our own.

If there is a current movement or direction in making a contemporary home, it is a movement against uniformity and design-by-formula. The perfect-white-box ideal, for example, can work brilliantly in some circumstances – usually as a solution for uncompromising minimalists with big budgets – but this approach can diminish the individuality of a place and flatten out its meaning. The alternative, working with what exists and not a preconception of an end result, is a celebration of the experience of a place.

Acknowledging the original function and design of a building as a positive asset, and incorporating or interpreting this in any structural changes or plans to regenerate or update a space, demonstrates an enjoyment of juxtaposition that is an essential aspect of an ancient and modern aesthetic.

The ideas and solutions presented in this chapter demonstrate how to combine ancient and modern in a way that celebrates and uses the original structural elements of a building. A selection of different examples shows how to adapt or incorporate original architectural features in a positive and dynamic way so that they do not predetermine an overall design aesthetic. For example, a sculptural custom-designed contemporary house can accommodate an enriching collection of heritage furniture, artefacts and textiles in a series of bold juxtapositions. Equally, it is possible to repair the original structure of an eighteenth-century town house and create a light, welcoming, comfortable contemporary environment which avoids any sense that the past is being re-created as an exercise in historical correctness.

A+M

RIGHT Bare floorboards and white walls, ceilings and window frames simplify and update the structure of this eighteenth-century town house in east London, and provide a pared-down environment for flea-market furniture and art.
OPPOSITE The curving wall in this converted spice warehouse in New York is an imaginative architectural feature that separates a kitchen from eating and relaxing areas in an open-plan space.

New living spaces

Ten years ago the age and style of a building's exterior was a good indication of the configuration of the space and overall aesthetic within it. This is definitely no longer the case. Just as for all kinds of social, economic and cultural reasons there is no typical family unit and no typical working day, there is no longer any easy way of categorizing a home. Architectural terms like 'open-plan', 'multifunctioning' and 'integration of indoor and outdoor space' apply equally to such diverse properties as a 1960s maisonette, a Victorian artisan's cottage or an expansive industrial conversion.

Essentially, the place you live in is either a purpose-built domestic building of some kind or a conversion from a non-domestic space. Examples of domestic architecture such as historic houses, modern developments in period or contemporary style, apartments and, increasingly, custom-designed houses on any suitable site with planning permission, are all recognizable fixtures in every rural and urban landscape in the Western world. And while most domestic architecture consists of convenient, practical structures whose design and proportions are familiar, if conventional, it also offers excellent potential to create individual contemporary homes.

There are many different ways to adapt and update existing domestic architecture. As well as dismantling what exists and reinventing domestic space, it is possible to transform a structure

Orientating a relaxing area between a row of big windows and classical-style support columns in this New York loft acknowledges the positive and original structure of the space and makes good use of available light. A wall of book shelves with window insets creates an appealing light-well effect.

beyond recognition with simple and inexpensive modifications. And while domestic properties still make up the biggest proportion of housing options, conversions of non-domestic buildings are providing more and more places to live. These include former factories, railway depots, schools, offices and churches. The fact that the buildings appear on the market in the first place reveals a lot about important changes in our communities – urban regeneration, downsizing of commercial premises and the increase in working from home that has been made possible by computers. Often in central urban locations, buildings like these offer the potential to develop alternative living spaces that are very different, both externally and internally, to those provided by conventional domestic architecture.

As well as introducing a whole new concept and understanding of what a contemporary home can look like, conversions are exerting a powerful influence on domestic architecture in general. The new vocabulary and expectation of space, light, openness and even industrial fixtures and fittings is spilling over into conventional buildings. (Loft-style is so popular that some new developments are built to look like former industrial spaces and claim to offer this type of accommodation.) With such diversity in the housing market it is impossible to apply any kind of preset design formula. Certainly, a conventional apartment or house is very different to an industrial conversion – yet both have positive original assets.

Assessing your space
If you are contemplating any structural changes begin with a comprehensive assessment of your options and yourself. Big issues to think about are how to make the most of the space in your home, cost efficiency and how the changes will improve the quality of your life.

An essential part of this assessment is information about yourself and the people you live with. Whether you live with one other person or a group of individuals or are part of a family it is important to take everyone's requirements into account. This is basic building-block information and will indicate how best to organize space and areas for change or improvement. If you have children think about their possible future requirements. For example, include in your plans the option to create a space for them, away from parents or other family members, as they grow older and more independent.

Look at your home objectively and note any positive or negative features. Find out about the age and origin of the building. This will help you appreciate the configuration of its space and the materials it was built from. Are there any fittings and fixtures or architectural features that are specific to the structure? Draw a plan and note the general layout and positions of facilities and utilities. Look at the way you use the overall space and how it facilitates, or possibly limits, the way you live. Think about the different rooms in terms of their size, quality of light and where they are, and decide which functions they are best suited for. Map out the routes people take when they move from one part of the building to another and note any inconvenient restrictions or points of congestion.

Getting the basic structure and layout right is worth time and effort. However, structural solutions are not always without compromise. For example, it may be necessary to specify wooden window frames in place of metal ones to keep within budget. Plan to get the framework right and then specify the best materials you can afford.

It is equally important to consider how any changes you make will affect the essence of the building. For example, in Langland and Bell's low-key update of an historic house in London, or Alastair Gordon and Barbara de Vries' conversion of an industrial space in New Jersey, both solutions are a response to the essential character of a building. Simplifying and reducing a structure will often achieve this without taking away the authenticity of a place.

Once the framework of the building is right you can create the ambience you want by adding furniture and details like a rug or a textile, or by painting a wall.

Changing the structure

To see the potential for change in your home, take an overview and think of it as a unit that defines an amount of space and contains an amount of light. Each unit is built from a combination of walls, floors, ceilings and windows in a variety of materials such as concrete, wood, glass, stone, metal and brick. Its shape is usually determined by where it is built: it may stand alone on its own site, in a line-up or terrace or in a stack or block with other units of the same or varying size.

The volume of space within each unit is usually rigid or set. Sometimes it is possible to add space by extending sideways, upwards or downwards. For example, when buying the top floor of an office building in east London to convert it into an apartment, designer Fiona Naylor also bought 'air rights' or permission to add another level to the existing structure. The roof extension is a glass and metal construction in contrast to the heavy-duty 1950s light-industrial architecture below. With cross-London views and an outside play area for her children, the extension is like a massive light box and transforms the whole space.

It is sometimes possible to use previously unusable space, for example by converting a basement or the space under a roof. If these areas do not have enough height for day-to-day use, a basement is a useful storage or laundry area and a roof space converts to an ideal sleeping platform. However, even without extending an existing structure, it is possible to manipulate and optimize the perception and experience of space.

The level of light within a unit is dependent on light coming in and circulating effectively. Note where it enters and how it moves around throughout the day. Is the space light and airy? Is it possible to add extra windows or skylights, or take out or reduce a wall that is blocking light? Any area with good light is welcoming – ideal for a key activity like relaxing, eating or working.

Basic standards and controls apply to all levels of structural change, so it is essential to follow regulations. Always contact the relevant planning and engineering departments or building regulators before making alterations. Also check utilities and service systems as these are subject to controls. Know where water pipes and electricity cables run and avoid or reroute them if possible.

Finding out about any restrictions or regulations that concern the building you live in will give a good indication of the scope of possibilities. For example, it may be impossible to alter the design of a window in a nineteenth-century house for reasons of historic preservation. If a building is listed as being of special architectural interest it is important to obtain permission before making structural alterations to the interior. In a twentieth-century building with multiple occupancy you may not be allowed to remove a concrete staircase because of fire regulations. However, it is sometimes possible to negotiate a solution or an alternative plan.

Conservation and planning regulations frequently restrict the extent to which changes can be made to the street-facing facades of buildings, to ensure that they remain architecturally compatible with adjacent ones. However, there is often greater freedom to change the rear of a property, away from the general view. If this is the case, it may be possible to totally remodel a structure behind a street-facing facade.

If you plan to adapt or restructure a building, or if you are looking for a property to work on, get professional help. A good architect's skills include spatial awareness, experience and the ability to see a job through to completion with a proper plan of action. He or she will also have the vision to assess the potential as well as the reality of a property. Engineers, surveyors and planners offer expertise and advice in all technical matters. If you plan to introduce openings or internal windows, add mezzanine levels or remove part of a floor, the structure of the building may require further support and strengthening by inserting an additional beam. The strength of the beam will depend on the weight it will have to bear or how many floors there are above it.

Some non-domestic conversions can tolerate extensive alterations without requiring additional strengthening. This is because of the industrial standards and specifications of the original construction. For example, when architects Fernlund and Logan converted two floors of an industrial building in New York it was possible to create a double-height living area without additional supports.

Possible options for structural changes include radical alterations, a fusion of what exists with something new, and low-key simplification and rationalization.

LEFT Converting this sixteenth-century barn into a studio workspace required low-key changes to the original structure, for example cementing glass panels into ventilation slots in the original stone wall. **OPPOSITE** Using architectural salvage, including a staircase and panelling from a nineteenth-century building, designer Frederic Mechiche has re-worked the layout of his Paris apartment.

In his radical redesign of the interior of a four-bedroom Edwardian house, architect J.F. Delsalle has removed every original structural element to create a contemporary open-plan environment with a powerful sense of space and light.

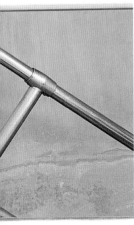

Radical alterations

The radical option is about extreme restructuring – dismantling or rejecting most of what exists to reinvent a very different environment. In architect Richard Rogers' well-known conversion and amalgamation of two terrace houses in London, the facade of the building is all that remains of the original structure. Inside his family home the main living area is a magnificent space with a double-height ceiling that extends across the width of two houses. Daylight circulates without the obstruction of the former walls and floors, and as a result the sense of light and space within the building is extraordinary.

Where Richard Rogers subverts the concept of a conventional house with fantastic dimensions and uncustomary views within the space, architect John Pawson's conversion of a modest period town house – also in an inner London location – follows a pattern that is typical of many similar buildings, with a kitchen and dining area in the basement, a sitting room on the ground floor, main sleeping and bathing areas on the first floor and children's bedrooms on the second floor. However, his radical restructuring behind the original facade includes a dynamic staircase that spans two levels in a single diagonal line and liberates valuable living space. An industrial-standard steel frame supports stone floors on every level and a stone bath next to the main bedroom.

In both properties the juxtaposition between original and modern architecture is incisive. Their facades give no clue to the restructuring within. Yet in both cases domestic buildings that date from a very different era to ours have been effectively adapted to provide original environments for contemporary families.

With conventional homes the challenge is often how to reorder a traditional layout of rooms to create greater openness and integration. With non-domestic conversions it is often the exact opposite. The challenge is how to divide space without detracting from a sense of openness, without obstructing light and preventing it from penetrating into the middle of the space, and without imposing an inappropriate domestic layout.

In the conversion by Fernlund and Logan mentioned on page 42 the solution was to maximize daylight by replacing the original factory windows with a glass wall and then to arrange activities around it. The main living area is a double-height space on the first level with magnificent views, thanks to this feature. The sleeping and bathing areas range around the central well from a gallery on the second level.

In architect Nik Randall's conversion of a former Victorian schoolhouse in London, contemporary mezzanines with open-tread staircases fit within the original structure like single freestanding constructions. There are junctions and juxtapositions where these and the original structure connect. The mezzanine levels sit on metal beams that in turn fix onto the original oak beams, but these junctions are kept to a minimum. Where the floor of the sleeping-mezzanine level joins the original structure a border of glass underlines both the separation and the connection between the two.

Introducing galleries or mezzanines and removing parts of floors are radical architectural changes and are relevant to all kinds of structures. Whether you take on an existing domestic space and adapt it, or convert a non-domestic unit, imaginative design and planning can create a dynamic new environment. However, a project of this kind requires vision, commitment, determination – and a big budget. It is less expensive to custom-design and build a new house than radically restructure an existing one of a similar size.

The fusion of old and new

The fusion option is less radical. It is about finding ways to work within an existing structure, or extend part of it, in order to modernize or customize existing space. These include adding an extension, replacing a staircase, taking away or cutting back solid walls, inserting a skylight or introducing sliding partitions.

Architects Azman Owens' reinterpretation of a modest Victorian terrace house in London took the existing layout of the rooms as a starting point. Most of the original walls remain in place to define different living areas. The changes the architects made, such as inserting internal windows and widening doorways, add to an overall sense of openness and connection within the space. A contemporary extension in the rear garden has a glass roof and seems open to the sky. It provides a direct contrast to the original structure, which has a welcoming sense of enclosure.

Azman Owens' use of high-specification materials like glass and stone alongside original floorboards and weather-beaten brickwork is a solution that offers a powerful juxtaposition of ancient and modern elements. Recycling or salvaging architectural materials and fixtures and fittings is an alternative option that is appropriate to historically correct restorations. A cow shed in Cornwall, converted by architect Jonathan Ball and Hugh Lander, an historic building adviser, is an example of this type of project. Historically and geographically correct roof slates and stone from a local derelict building were used in the restoration of the original structure and in a new extension that adjoins the cow shed at right angles.

The original building is now split into two levels with two bedrooms and a bathroom on the lower level and a third bedroom, shower room and gallery area on the one above. The extension forms a double-height open-plan living space for cooking, eating and relaxing. Ingeniously, the new walls comprise a layer of inexpensive breeze blocks behind a layer of authentic stone. They provide good insulation and mimic the depth and resonance of the original walls, so the new window and door recesses appear equal to the original ones.

An example of less conventional yet no less ingenious recycling is the conversion of what had been a commercial space in midtown Manhattan by architects Lot/ek. A single structural device intersects the space diagonally, and effectively separates living and working areas. The device is the aluminium siding of a container truck, cut into different sections that pivot, rotate or open upwards to reveal a compact kitchen and shower and provide access to a sleeping area. A wooden frame supports the siding, yet the effect is of a truck sliding through a building. The installation is in keeping with the raw industrial fittings and fixtures, which include concrete floors and surface piping, and is inventive, functional and strangely poetic. The art of this kind of juxtaposition is to bring out the essence of a place, and its success is often dependent upon the clarity and texture of the original structure. In this case the bold, raw state of the original building was equal to the boldness of the architectural device – so neither dominates the space.

Wherever you live, refine and edit the original structure to present a simple single message – an authentic sense of place. Whatever you take away will strengthen what remains.

A freestanding wooden platform on support struts fixed to a new concrete floor makes a bold addition to the conversion of a nineteenth-century brick factory, without altering or connecting with the original structure of the building.

THIS PAGE Reducing the amount of furniture and objects in a space and unifying floors, walls and ceilings with colour, as in this early twentieth-century wooden house on Long Island, both simplifies an interior and brings the architecture into focus.

OPPOSITE The original architectural features in this 1920s Paris studio include a double-height window and internal terrace overlooking the main living and working area. Painting the walls and ceiling white enhances the sense of space and light and gives greater clarity to elements and objects.

Low-key changes

While reduction is vital for the fusion process, it is also an important part of making low-key changes. This option is about simplifying an environment and reducing it to what is essential. Even without removing any structural features, it is possible to manipulate what exists by reorganizing it – eliminating excessive furniture and clutter will go a long way to redefining a sense of place – or using colour to present it in a different way.

The use of a single paint colour unifies and simplifies a space as well as updating it. In designer Ann Shore's former Georgian home in east London every surface apart from the bare floorboards is plain white. Shore chose not to restore the original panelling or replace a missing fireplace, preferring the simple effectiveness of paint to harmonize odd sections of brickwork or skirting boards. As the house is inherently austere, white optimizes light and a sense of space. It also provides an excellent backdrop to a juxtaposition of mid-twentieth-century furniture and ethnic artefacts. Despite a lack of obvious conveniences such as central heating, Shore's home expresses an unquestionably modern spirit.

As in Shore's house, white maximizes an overall sense of light and space. Deep colours like black or inky blue blur boundaries and distances between walls, ceilings and floors. Lilac, pale green and anything neutral produces a mellow welcoming effect. Bright crisp colours like yellow, sky blue or minty green often intensify a sense of being enclosed and work well in moderation.

As well as simplifying a structure and diminishing obtrusive decorative elements, colour can highlight special features and add definition. For example, an ornate ceiling in blood red or regal purple can be dynamic in a plain white space. Most colours look good in a block but intense ones like bright orange or graphite work exceptionally well, creating a dramatic change of pace. A bright colour will draw attention to an element in a room, for example if it is painted on the wall around an original fireplace. Or it will direct attention away from a feature if it is used on the wall opposite it. Using different colours throughout a home can indicate changing activities: soothing blues, greens and lilacs for sleeping and bathing and livelier lemons or limes for cooking and eating.

Walls and doors

External walls and doors outline whole cities, streets and buildings. Since they are subject to controls and restrictions that prohibit radical alterations, they must essentially remain true to their original design. However, architectural changes to an existing structure are sometimes permitted at the back of a building. Replacing a solid brick wall in a former factory with glass sliding doors or adding a concrete box to a Victorian terrace house are examples.

Internal walls are essentially devices for division and separation, and doors provide access to a room or space. It is possible to remove or modify internal walls without subverting the qualities that attracted you to the building in the first place, although alterations like these are not always cost-efficient. If you plan to reduce or take away a structural wall it will be necessary to insert a steel, concrete or timber beam to take the weight of the floors above it. Even extending a doorway or an opening to the full height of the wall may mean that additional support is required. If a wall conceals electricity cables or water pipes these services will have to be rerouted, making the project more complex. If you add a fixed wall, possibly to subdivide a spacious loft, this can incorporate essential services – for example, power and water supplies to a kitchen or bathing area – and provide built-in storage.

Some changes, for example removing part of a wall or replacing it with a glass panel, widening a doorway or simply taking away the door, will make better use of existing space and optimize daylight. They will also add internal views and help to unify the interior. Alternatively, if you do not want to make structural changes or if they are prohibited by planning regulations, using light colours, reflective finishes and plain roller blinds will maximize the existing space and light in a low-key way.

Walls and doors do not have to be fixed in one place or follow conventional grid-like divisions of space. In a loft in downtown New York a floor-to-ceiling panel set diagonally across one corner of a room, with access on either side, conceals a work area from the living space. Oblong windows cut into the panel allow light to enter from each side.

Movable walls are ingenious functional devices and come in a variety of forms that include rotating, pivoting, sliding or folding sections in steel, wood, plastic or sandblasted glass – even a nylon sheet with a zip in it. Their big advantage is that they are flexible and give you the freedom to change and manipulate the overall space on a day-to-day basis or to adapt to changing circumstances. For example, a movable wall can be used to reveal and conceal a work area in a living/working environment, or to create an optional sleeping area in an open-plan space.

Laying bare original surfaces by exposing brickwork or wooden doors and panelling, or by stripping wallpaper down to plaster, provides context and texture for a domestic space and a juxtaposition with modern structural elements like glass or stainless-steel panels. In the ancient and modern apartment of architecture professor Nigel Coates the grand wooden doors were part-stripped to reveal layers of different paint colours and present a capsule history of decoration from the nineteenth century.

ABOVE A 500-piece bamboo wall links different areas in an open-plan London loft. Although not based on a traditional Japanese design, it adds contrasting texture, colour and form to a Japanese-inspired interior. OPPOSITE This dynamic curving wall contrasts with the original architecture of the space and divides a kitchen area from a living area. A geometric cut-away allows connecting views.

The big advantage of sliding walls and screens is that they are flexible. Shoji screens, which are fundamental to traditional Japanese interiors, are used in this open-plan London loft to make an enclosure for dining or sleeping. They also provide optional separation between the main sleeping and living areas.

A doorway can be a major architectural feature or provide a low-key transition between rooms. This doorway in a New York loft is a focal point of the space, with a low-level opening and ancient decorative wooden doors in a double-height white wall. It leads into a bedroom and interconnecting bathroom decorated with a Moroccan theme.

Fixed internal doors and walls delineate the proportions and logic of a space and, depending on the materials they are made from, indicate whether a room or area is private or public. These vast metal and glass doors suggest openness and connection even when they are closed, whereas the wooden doors beyond do not.

oors determine how different areas are connected or separated. For example, glass connection whereas solid ones provide complete separation.

The laid-bare structure of this barn in the grounds of ceramicist Rupert Spira's sixteenth-century farmhouse in Shropshire is now a studio/workshop. Part of the original structure has been divided into a separate room by creating a wall of horizontal planks. The main crossbeam is original.

The raw structure of this brick factory in New Jersey, with an exposed brick wall and industrial-size windows, is a key reason for living in this space. Restoring and exposing every structural element, laying a new concrete floor and installing a wood-burning stove all help to domesticate the space in a way that is in keeping with the original character of the building.

Installing eighteenth-century salvage wood panelling in this Paris apartment changes the configuration of the rooms and the position of the doors. Painting the panelling with matt white paint unifies it without covering up cracks in the wood and provides a compelling contrast with modern classic twentieth-century furniture.

Windows

Daylight is fundamental to our well-being and enlivens everything from plain white walls to a ceramic pot. However, the architectural style of a building determines the level of light within it, and it is not always possible – or desirable – to alter this. For example, small windows in a period cottage are characteristic of the style of the building, whereas large windows are typical of loft-style conversions. The level of incoming light and sense of openness to the world outside is very different in each space. It is important to find ways to work with an existing structure, orientating space to take account of daylight moving through it and balancing a sense of openness with a sense of enclosure and seclusion. Before altering existing windows or adding extra ones, consider how any changes will affect the space and your use of it.

In general, big window areas create light, welcoming spaces to live in, so add windows and make existing ones bigger if you can and if this is appropriate to your requirements and the style of the building. Solutions that will have a low impact on its structure are most likely to get planning approval. Even if front-facing windows are beyond repair planners will usually stipulate that you replace them with copies rather than change their style, in order to preserve the original facade. You are more likely to get planning approval for alterations to the rear of a building. Here you may be able to do something radical or ingenious with windows or sections of glass, either using these as a continuation of the existing architectural style or as a contrast to it. Adding a glass-and-concrete extension, replacing a section of wall with a glass panel or increasing the ratio of glass to frame in an existing window will have a positive impact by increasing the amount of daylight in your home.

Inserting a skylight in a flat or sloping roof creates a luminous well and is ideal for brightening the space in the core of a building or bringing light into one like a church or factory that was not originally designed as a home. A skylight above an existing stairwell in a roof-space conversion or in the middle of a large space with windows at either end creates a beam of light that will transform anything directly below it. Introducing any new source of daylight in this way can initiate a total rethink of a space by turning a previously unappealing low-light area into a dynamic and welcoming one.

Consider windows as integral to the structure of a building and keep them plain. In a Georgian house painting the sash windows, shutters and wooden panelling pale grey unites and simplifies the structural elements in a room and draws attention to its proportions, creating a sense of order and space. Even an imposing Victorian bay window becomes less dominant if the frame is the same colour as the walls and ceiling. In a pared-down interior any architectural style or size of window, for example steel-pivot windows in an industrial space or even a decorative rose window in the conversion of a former church, will benefit from simple presentation and create a bold juxtaposition of ancient structural elements with a contemporary environment.

FROM LEFT TO RIGHT
The original floorboards in this early twentieth-century beach house come under heavy use from wet and sandy feet. Paint is a low-maintenance option for updating, recolouring and protecting them.
In this eighteenth-century priest's house in Yorkshire a pared-down aesthetic focuses attention on structural elements like an archway, wide door and natural stone floor in the main hall.
Reworking an interior is an opportunity to juxtapose flooring materials. Here stone slabs in a hallway lead into dark hardwood planks in a general living area, underlining the different uses of the space.
Inserting borders or patterns into a floor by using a contrasting material, such as these mosaic tiles in concrete, can enliven an expanse of uniform flooring.
Traditional Japanese tatami mats introduce a soft, natural texture to an area. In this oriental-inspired space they also provide an alternative base for a futon.
In this New York loft underfloor heating transforms a concrete floor into a comfortable area for low-level relaxing on a horseshoe arrangement of cushions.
Exposing original floorboards in ancient buildings can reveal appealing inconsistencies, like the misaligned floorboards in this nineteenth-century house.

Floors

A floor is integral not just to the structure of a space but to its look and feel. Essentially they provide a base to any given level, separate multiple levels and sometimes demarcate different functional areas. The flooring material can provide a harmonious base to unite all other elements or be used to create juxtapositions with the style of architecture and furniture. The textures and colours of different materials transmit a whole range of visual and sensory messages that influence our perception and enjoyment of a place. For example, an expanse of concrete with underfloor heating is no less cocooning in its own way than a woollen carpet, but it suggests a very different use of space. Hard and structural, it directs attention to the quality of light or openness in a space and draws a bold line under any furniture, object or work of art. A carpet, by comparison, is a soft furnishing that brings the entire floor into use as a place to sit or lie on in comfort.

The key options for floors are to expose and possibly repair an original one, to install an alternative – perhaps on top of the original – or to introduce a floor covering.

Exposing an original stone, wood or concrete floor is a way to acknowledge an authentic detail. Concrete as a backdrop to American country furniture, for example, will provide a powerful juxtaposition of ancient and modern elements. If an original floor requires extensive repair it is possible to make a feature of this by using contrasting new and old materials, such as bright plastic filler to plug holes in worn wooden boards, or concrete to replace missing slate tiles.

Replacing a floor or installing a new one provides an opportunity to manipulate the impact of different materials on existing architecture. Salvaged floorboards in a contemporary interior, or plywood sheets cut into oversized blocks in a traditional one, are cost-efficient solutions. Glass flooring on a mezzanine level will allow light to penetrate to the area below. Other options include concrete, stone, slate, marble, brick, stainless steel and ceramic or quarry tiles. Some materials, like stone and glass, are best left in a raw state. Wood and concrete are receptive to different finishes such as matt or gloss varnish, paint or resin.

Floor coverings include cork, linoleum, coir, rubber, seagrass and carpet. Any of these options provides opportunities for juxtaposition or connection with the structure of a space, or can help to simplify or update it in preparation for ancient and modern furniture and details.

If insulation against noise and loss of heat is a priority – this applies especially in apartments – it is possible to inject or insert buffer materials into structural cavities or raise a wooden floor on rubber pads. These installations are becoming less expensive so are worth investigating as an alternative to wall-to-wall carpeting. As a low-tech solution, inserting either string or wood pulp and glue in the gaps between floorboards will reduce noise and heat loss.

Finally, a note of caution. Changing an existing floor is disruptive and represents a major investment. It is important to consider the impact different options will have on the structure, appearance and overall feel of your home. It is also essential to think about any changes you may wish to make in the future and choose a type of floor that will be flexible enough to work with these.

Stairs

A staircase is the spine of a building and provides essential connection between different levels. How it looks and relates to other structural elements, how it demarcates and uses space, how it links different levels, how it affects light and even how it sounds when you walk on it are all factors that will contribute to the aesthetic of your home.

As with any original feature, it is important to review what exists before making alterations. With a period staircase the right decision is often to leave well alone. (If it is of special historic or architectural interest building regulations will prevent you changing it.) In this case, integrating a staircase into a general living area – fire regulations permitting – by removing internal walls or widening a doorway gives visual and physical access to an important architectural feature and provides a dramatic focus in a laid-bare space.

Check an old staircase for safety and repair it if necessary. However, it is often counterproductive and not cost-efficient to undertake a full good-as-new restoration. Worn wooden stair treads and banisters, or layer upon layer of paint, provide clues to years of use and add an individuality that would be diminished if the stairs were restored. If you opt to paint them, possibly to integrate them with an overall colour scheme, use rubber paint or several coats of floor paint with a hardwearing varnish to even out any minor fractures in the wood and combat splinters or nail heads. Wax the original wooden handrails as a contrast to the colour. An alternative to painting the stairs is to cover the treads with neutral flooring like linoleum or rubber tiles.

If you plan to install a new staircase, possibly because the original one is beyond repair or you need to access new levels, think about the visual impact as well as the safety aspects of different options. For example, an industrial steel-mesh staircase is a dynamic architectural feature, either in a loft-style apartment or in contrast to a conventional domestic interior, and allows light to penetrate to the space beneath. Even basic metal treads and a tubular steel handrail put together with scaffolding fixings can be every bit as impressive as a traditional design in oak.

BELOW LEFT A standard-issue industrial staircase using cost-efficient tubular steel and open metal treads provides a dynamic disjuncture with the architectural style of this Edwardian family house and its decorative ancient and modern furniture.
BELOW RIGHT The design and construction of this Gothic staircase in a church conversion make it a dominant feature. (Unusually, the stairs lead to the former chapel.) Keeping the rest of the area plain and light balances the historic architectural feature.

Integrating a staircase into a general living area by removing internal walls or widening a doorway gives visual and physical access to an important architectural feature.

This sweeping wood and wrought-iron staircase in a Paris apartment is a piece of architectural salvage. Its elegant form and light, worn treads connect with the shape of the Barcelona chair and the patina of its worn leather.

Architectural features

Features such as fireplaces, architraving, ceiling roses, wood panelling and wrought-iron balustrading chronicle the design, construction and evolution of a building. They provide a link to a particular period or to the building's original use, and their relevance to an ancient and modern environment is to add context and a sense of place.

However, it is essential to find a balance between past and present to avoid overwhelming a space with excessive detail and history. Emphasizing a single, simple feature sometimes has far more resonance than leaving everything in place. In a loft apartment, keeping only the industrial steel loading-bay doors provides a reminder of what the structure was used for and adds texture and contrast.

Original features can be diminished by insensitive conversions. For example, the impact of an ornate ceiling is reduced by the insertion of a partition wall. Removing the wall will restore the ceiling as a feature and reinstate a sense of proportion to the space.

Consider the condition of architectural features when deciding which to retain and which to remove or replace. For example, if a section of decorative coving is in less than perfect condition do you remove it, restore it or leave it as it is? Coving often conceals

gaps in the plaster where the walls meet the ceiling so removing it would involve plastering them in. Copying and restoring it could be expensive, although in a building of historic interest planning regulations sometimes require this. So leaving the coving as it is may well be the solution. However, giving a bold or decorative feature unnecessary prominence can undermine the unity of a pared-down environment.

It can be difficult to be objective about what to keep and repair because of the values we give to our architectural heritage. Yet values change and it is best to assess features in terms of how they fit in with a contemporary style. A modest timber-frame-and-brick farmworker's cottage with an open fireplace and stone hearth is now a premium space precisely because of its original construction and plain architectural features. On the other hand, a grand feature like a Victorian Gothic built-in oak bookcase, which once stood for wealth and social importance, is of much less value today and could be given less prominence by painting it the same colour as the walls.

Creating a space with an ancient and modern aesthetic will help you to make decisions about all the structural elements in your home and direct you towards a total concept that reflects your own style.

ABOVE LEFT A wrap-around white space with white walls and ceilings and terrazzo flooring contribute to the visual impact of this restored marble fireplace in an 1860 New York house. ABOVE RIGHT A low-key fire surround with inset blue-grey slate tiles and giant Scottish beach pebbles is the focus of this bathroom, which has a Japanese-style cedarwood bath. The colours and materials combine to create a mellow, natural environment. OPPOSITE Set flat into bare pink plaster walls, this architectural salvage Gothic stone fireplace is one of a pair in an open-plan living area. A contemporary glitter painting hangs on the wall between them.

Industrial conversion

A CONTEMPORARY REWORKING OF A NINETEENTH-CENTURY BRICK FACTORY

LEFT The wooden mezzanine is supported by raw-looking diagonal wooden struts fixed together with locally made metal brackets. This low-tech installation is freestanding within the original walls and connects with the concrete floor for rigidity. **BELOW LEFT** The low-tech staircase is made out of aluminium T-bars with ash treads. Its open design optimizes the sense of connection between different levels without blocking light. **MAIN PICTURE** The area underneath the 3-metre-high installation is an open-plan living space. The kitchen area consists of stainless-steel fittings and appliances, which provide a contrast to the original brickwork.

A former brick factory in New Jersey, built in 1894, is now the family home of Alastair Gordon, Barbara de Vries and their children. With the input of friends and architects Henry Smith-Miller and Laurie Hawkinson, the couple took on a dilapidated building and began a three-year project of restoration and conversion.

Despite its industrial origins and plain construction, the factory is a handsome building. Its imposing shape, size and orientation, and the proportion and position of its windows, suggest a classical style of architecture. The biggest challenge in converting the space was turning it into a home without losing sight or sense of the original structure. The solution was to install bold contemporary architectural

structures in the interior and leave the brick exterior and windows intact. The living space at the heart of the building is now ingeniously divided on two levels: the ground floor and a wooden mezzanine. The architecture and construction of the mezzanine is deliberately raw and temporary-looking, to fuse with the bare brick walls and concrete floor of the space. Yet this simple division has been the key to transforming a vast area designed to house industrial equipment into an individual home compatible with the requirements of a professional creative couple and their young family.

The building is entered through a grand glass-and-metal doorway that leads directly into a large workshop/studio. This remains in a relatively raw state and may be developed in the future. A wall of semitransparent sliding plastic panels divides the overall space in half, with the workshop/studio on one side and a spacious open-plan living area on the other.

Introducing the mezzanine provided a logical division to the open-plan space, with an integrated area for cooking, eating and relaxing on the ground floor and sleeping, bathing and working areas above. The mezzanine is a 3-metre-high platform made from timber crossbeams with plywood panels for flooring, surrounded by a wooden railing and a transparent screen made from bullet-proof plastic – all inexpensive industrial materials. The whole structure is supported on struts fixed to the concrete floor with aluminium footings.

The general living space underneath the platform includes a children's area, an interconnecting bathroom and a separate office behind permanent divisions, but in essence the ground floor is open-plan. The kitchen consists of low-level industrial shelving units between a cooker, dishwasher and stainless-steel sink unit. The work surface is blue stone and a stainless-steel splashback runs the length of the kitchen area with additional open shelving. In keeping with the structure of the building, this is a good-looking, hard-working area with no decoration or excessive detailing. It demonstrates the confident and resourceful fusion of ancient and modern throughout the space.

It was essential to create separate spaces on the mezzanine, specifically for the adults' and children's sleeping areas and the bathroom. Installing a combination of fixed and sliding plywood panels to divide the area without losing a sense of space was an inexpensive and low-impact solution.

All the architectural features and materials in this imaginative project are cost-efficient and resourceful and the mezzanine is the most obvious example of this approach. There are many other examples of inventive design. The lightweight plastic panels that divide the main workshop/studio and living spaces are one of the key structural elements, providing insulation and separation without blocking essential light. On the mezzanine level, identical panels fixed to a beam with pins effectively screen an office. The staircase to the mezzanine level is made of aluminium T-bars with ash steps, and the roof insulation is hidden with metres of iridescent fireproof membrane.

Like everything else in this exceptional space, the mix of furniture and objects reflects an appreciation of both basic low-cost solutions and one-off investment pieces. Contemporary aluminium clip-on spotlights hanging from the mezzanine, an ancient African daybed and a set of Windsor chairs designed in the 1950s are good examples of this policy.

BELOW The upper level is predominantly a family space for sleeping, bathing, playing and relaxing. Sliding plywood panels, hanging from a wooden frame, provide optional divisions and enclosure.
OPPOSITE LEFT AND BELOW RIGHT Well-chosen fixtures and fittings in the bathing area, including a child-friendly basin, look too good to conceal so the sliding panel stays open when not in use. Two well-placed mirrors reflect light and extend the space with views of ancient and modern architectural juxtapositions.
OPPOSITE ABOVE RIGHT Semitransparent plastic panels pinned to a beam provide a low-tech division between an office and general family space. The panels blur the visual impact of office equipment and storage without blocking essential light from the inner areas.

Modernization and connection

RESTRUCTURING AN EDWARDIAN ARTIST'S STUDIO AND A GEORGIAN COTTAGE

BELOW This view shows the roof of the Edwardian studio on the right and the Georgian cottage in the background.
RIGHT Taken inside the former studio at ground level, this photograph shows the cooking and dining areas. The front door of the cottage is at the end of the passage on the left.

This imaginative and radical architectural transformation updates two modest historic buildings in London and joins them to make a single dynamic contemporary space. The project by architects Stickland Coombe involved gutting, remodelling and refurbishing the studio and cottage, increasing the incoming light and introducing high-specification materials to unify the structure and create an area for living and working. While the structure within is now radically modern, the street-facing facades of the two buildings remain the same.

In the Edwardian studio, which was rented by Charles Rennie Mackintosh between 1915 and 1928, a monolithic blank white wall is a dynamic focal point, both in the main living area and in the overall space. As an architectural feature, it hangs from the original roof of the studio and

The studio is now an expansive living and entertaining space. A new skylight in the roof brings light into the barn-like structure. The owner collects contemporary art and the monolithic wall above the fireplace is used for film screenings.

The architects' radical scheme works with the original shape and historic context of the buildings.

OPPOSITE This view shows the interior of the cottage, looking towards the former studio. The passage leading into the main living area is lined with cupboards for essential storage. The stairs on the left lead to a mezzanine work area.
ABOVE LEFT A traditionally shaped bath with plain feet and a mono-block tap presents a dynamic profile, visible from the bed, that makes no concession to historic style.
ABOVE CENTRE A new staircase leads down to the main hallway, and French windows provide access to a compact roof terrace.
ABOVE RIGHT The upper level of the cottage now comprises open-plan sleeping and bathing areas. A change of colour compounds the change in scale from the living and working area downstairs and adds to the sense of enclosure and privacy.

magnifies and celebrates its asymmetrical apex. As a practical device, it conceals storage for glassware and entertainment equipment, houses a flue for a contemporary gas fire and provides a permanent blank screen for film projection.

Opposite the wall, looking towards the cottage, the apex of the roof forms part of a geometric jigsaw of cut-aways and openings. On the ground level the cut-away and opening on the right are part of the kitchen area. The opening on the left leads out towards the cottage and main entrance. The cut-away triangle on the upper level is a mezzanine work area with a fitted work table and storage.

The level of light in the studio, which houses a collection of photographs and contemporary paintings by British artists, was an important consideration, so a new skylight was added and existing ones were modified. The skylights also illuminate the blank wall and create shadows on either side.

A wide hall leading from the original front door of the cottage to the studio beyond forms a bold link between the two buildings and provides full-length front-to-back views of the space. A circular skylight is a luminous architectural feature in the centre and adds a dynamic geometric shape to a series of openings and cut-aways – access to the entire interior radiates from this point. The main living area is directly ahead. The axis of the hall and a sense of space and light ahead work together to draw you into this impressive open-plan

area. A row of ten identical doors lining the wall on the right conceals a boiler and hot-water tank and a comprehensive storage system. To the left there is a separate bedroom and shower room and the stairs to a mezzanine working area. This has views over the main living space. To the right there is a reading room and new stairs to the upper level of the cottage.

The traditional Georgian cottage, which originally had a central staircase, retains a sense of enclosure in contrast to the openness of the studio and provides a logical environment for bedrooms and a reading room. There are two separate rooms on the ground level, while the upper level is now a spacious interconnecting bedroom and bathroom with access to a roof terrace.

Despite this open-plan arrangement the upper-level space is in complete contrast to the main living and working area in terms of size, simplicity and colour. Moving the stairs and making the area open-plan were relatively simple structural changes. The prominent architectural feature is a storage unit which separates the bathroom and stairs.

The challenge was to combine two very different structures – Georgian and Edwardian – with very different original functions – domestic building and artist's studio – to make a coherent and enjoyable contemporary space to live and work in. The architects' radical scheme works with the original shape and historic context of the buildings to create a spacious, light and welcoming home.

Simplification

REINVENTING AN EIGHTEENTH-CENTURY TOWN HOUSE

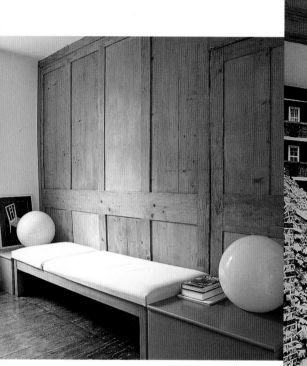

From the outside this modest terraced town house is unprepossessing. The only indication of the sensitive reworking within it is the historic grey paint on the original frames of the sash windows.

Built in 1790 in the East End of London, the Georgian house is on four levels including a basement and a roof space. The owners, artists Ben Langlands and Nikki Bell, were drawn to it because both the house and the neighbourhood are rich in history and culture, so it was essential that any alterations did not detract from the building's origins. The house is tall and narrow – a quarter of the width is taken up with stairs and hallways screened by a single wall of Georgian panelling that runs the full height of the structure – so

ABOVE LEFT A former doctor's examination couch with cut-down legs and a linen-covered mattress makes a snug reading area on the ground floor.
ABOVE RIGHT The original plain eighteenth-century panelling screens the hallway and stairs on every level. Apart from the exhibition space on the second floor, the panelling is waxed and provides a warm soft backdrop to every room.
OPPOSITE The all-white scheme on the second floor provides a permanent exhibition space for the artists' work, which includes monochrome installations like these chairs.

ABOVE The original
dividing wall between
the bedroom and
bathroom on the top
floor remains but on
every other level it has
been removed to
optimize openness.
RIGHT New skylights
above the bed and bath
increase natural light,
which is magnified by
an all-white policy,
and create a bright,
welcoming private area.
BELOW Access to the
bathroom is either
through the bedroom or
via an original door in
the wooden panelling.

optimizing a sense of space and light was a key objective. The original arrangement of two separate rooms back-to-back on every level, each with a window and fireplace, has been altered by removing the interior dividing walls on the three lower levels. This provides single areas that extend the full length of the house with a window at either end to maximize natural light. In the roof space a section of the original dividing wall remains to partly separate a bedroom and bathroom. New skylights increase natural light.

All the original architectural detailing such as doors, panelling, fire surrounds and skirting boards is plain, which provided a good basis for creating a pared-down environment. Introducing a minimalist colour code – all the floors and walls are either white or original wood – simplified and reduced the structure of the house to a series of horizontal and vertical planes. Yet given the patina of age and wear of the materials – all the surfaces are wonderfully imperfect – the overall effect of a minimal contemporary space within an historic structure is a celebration of ancient and modern.

This is the poetry of a scheme like this: to reduce the architecture to what is essential without diminishing a sense of history. Keeping furniture and objects to a minimum supports this approach and avoids overcrowding. Dedicating each level to a separate function – cooking and eating in the basement, relaxing on the ground floor, an exhibition or installation area on the second floor and sleeping and bathing at the top – facilitates the whole process of rationalization and simplification.

In the basement the only source of light at the front of the house is provided by pavement lights, while French windows that open onto a courtyard garden boost light levels at the back. The floor in the basement is concrete but looks like ancient stone. An efficient line-up of kitchen appliances and storage units along a single wall, and glass-fronted cabinets on either side of the chimneys for storing tableware, leave the space relatively free. There are two tables – an original office table and a copy of this, which can be used separately or combined to form a line or square, depending on requirements.

The relaxing area on the ground floor has an appealing arrangement of found furniture including a one-arm sofa and a doctor's examination couch. Like most pieces in the house, they come from local skips. They have been updated and transformed with low-key adjustments: the sofa is covered with linen, and the legs of the couch have been shortened. A circular table and country chairs provide an alternative place for reading.

The second floor is an important exhibition area for the artists' work, which includes monochromatic displays such as white chairs and tables. In keeping with these pieces, this is the only room where the Georgian panelling has been painted white. The top floor is a white-out haven (apart from the original Georgian panelling) for sleeping and bathing.

Certainly the house is minimal, yet every level presents a different combination of finish and materials as well as function, and the minor adjustments and alterations have had considerable impact.

The view from the bath, looking back to the bedroom, shows how gloss and matt finishes on walls, floors and doors enliven a plain colour scheme with reflections and variation.

A+m

FUNCTION

'Taking the simple approach allows scope for self-expression and for creating an environment which will continue to work and give pleasure.'
Sir Terence Conran

THIS PAGE Efficient planning, which makes the most of space and natural light, creates a practical, welcoming environment for combinations of ancient and modern. In this kitchen stainless-steel storage cupboards and white kitchen units are contrasted with a limed-oak floor and antique table and chairs. **PREVIOUS PAGES** Installing sliding shoji screens in a traditional Japanese-style tatami room provides optional separation within an open-plan loft space.

A contemporary home is both a sanctuary and the environment in which we relax, cook, eat, sleep, bathe and possibly work. If you have children it is also where they will play and explore the world around them as they grow up.

Organizing a home so that it functions efficiently on a day-to-day basis therefore involves making practical, cost-efficient and ergonomic decisions – about such issues as the kind of work surface that is right for a kitchen, how to provide enough storage in a living room and where to position a single chair and an adjustable light for reading. Yet how an interior looks and feels is equally important to our enjoyment and well-being: a plaster wall painted in a pale colour will enhance a feeling of space, while the worn texture of an antique country table will bring warmth to a streamlined modern kitchen. Acknowledging a sense of place and balancing this acknowledgment with the requirements of contemporary life is the key principle of an ancient and modern aesthetic. Basing your decisions on this principle will enable you to create a functional space that is individual to you and enjoyable to live in.

Practical decisions about where different functions and activities take place within a home depend on individual requirements and preferences. However, the logic of a building's architectural style and original features often suggests how the space could be used and presents powerful reasons for a certain kind of organization. When you assess the potential function of a room or area its proportions, the level of daylight within it, its position in relation to the overall space and any significant decorative features like a fireplace or ornate ceiling are all important factors to consider. Conventional concepts about how to organize space also influence our decisions. Examples are sleeping on an upper floor rather than in a basement or close to a living area, bathing in a separate room and socializing or relaxing in the largest and most important space – one that often has architectural features like original panelling, a fireplace or big windows.

This chapter describes how a wide range of ancient and modern elements, from furniture to kitchen fittings, floor coverings to existing architectural features, can be combined to create spaces that are suited to specific functions and uses.

Relaxing

An impression of softness and a sense of sanctuary are essential elements in a relaxing area. Softness doesn't just mean soft furniture to sit or lie on; it means creating a cumulative effect with paint colours, floor coverings, furniture, textiles, lighting and accessories. Combine white walls and pale original floorboards in a nineteenth-century house with contemporary furniture and ancient ethnic artefacts and textiles, for example. Or use midtones like grey or pewter for walls, with dark brown or black flooring and an eclectic mix of contemporary artefacts and predominantly ancient furniture. Soft rugs or carpets, ambient lighting, and possibly curtains or blinds to modify incoming daylight and provide privacy, all contribute to a welcoming environment. Even if you sit on a hard chair at a table, lie in the bath watching television or read in bed more often than you sit on a sofa or in an easy chair, creating a personal haven is a positive step towards achieving a relaxed and enjoyable lifestyle.

Relaxing areas are conventionally where people meet and socialize. In domestic buildings living rooms are often bigger, lighter and grander than other areas, with finer finishes and architectural detailing to underline their importance. In an industrial conversion large windows or original structural features like the brick wall in a former Victorian factory often indicate the best location for an area to relax in.

Consider how you want to define a relaxing area, and what its focal point will be. An antique fireplace or a modern wood stove is a traditional and logical option. If an interior lacks features like these, use art objects, a painting, textiles or a block of colour on a wall to provide a focus within the space.

The next step is to plan how to orientate a mixture of ancient and modern elements like chairs, tables and lamps into a compatible and harmonious arrangement. Begin with the largest piece of furniture, perhaps a modern sofa or an antique cupboard for storing entertainment equipment. If there is more than one large element, find a balance between them and take account of any prominent architectural features. For example, in a sitting room with an original fireplace a traditional chesterfield sofa could be positioned to face the fireplace and a modern low-level teak and steel cabinet could be placed against a wall to one side of it. Experiment until you create a feeling of balance and order. Consider movement and access around any key elements – especially if room or cupboard doors open into an area – and how well the arrangement responds to different-sized groups of people, for example a couple or a gathering of friends using the area. This indicates where to place smaller items such as easy chairs and occasional tables and lamps.

ABOVE The design and central position of the metal staircase, in front of a dynamic wall of windows giving spectacular views of New York, indicates that this low-level relaxing area is of key importance in a studio space.
OPPOSITE This built-in bookcase contains, and imposes order on, a collection of books without detracting from the welcoming informality of the area. Graphic contemporary uplighters on the support pillar provide atmospheric lighting at night.

Big windows with a big view of the Thames and the London skyline provided a logical starting point for orientating and organizing this expansive loft space. The oriental sofa and chairs, set in a traditional arrangement around a low table, are appropriately generous and bold in size, shape and colour, and work well in this contemporary environment.

If an interior is open-plan, or if you want to use a space for more than one purpose – eating or working as well as relaxing, for example – create divisions with lighting, textiles, hangings or floor coverings, or position furniture so that it defines an area. In the conversion of a former upholstery workshop in London's East End an Arts and Crafts table with a display of magnificent ethnic figures and masks demarcates a relaxing area within an open-plan space. In a former spice warehouse in New York a contemporary modular sofa defines an L-shaped relaxing area, and in an artist's Art Deco studio in Paris an arrangement of two 1950s Bertoia lounging chairs with sheepskin cushions, and a low table and footstool with an ancient animal skin underfoot, effectively communicates intimacy and relaxation within an open-plan space.

A relaxing area is a multifunction space for activities like listening to music and reading, so storage and display space is needed for a wide range of items including hi-fis, CDs, videos or DVDs, books and magazines. Ancient and modern storage options include fitted and freestanding items. A period house might have original built-in shelves and cupboards. Alternatively, explore contemporary options such as white, wall-mounted low-level cabinets, which add an architectural feature and provide display space for ceramics or photographic prints. Freestanding storage options include modern low-level teak cabinets in an historic house or apartment, or an antique French armoire in a loft conversion.

Keeping everything in one place and possibly out of view, for example by using an antique country cupboard with peeling paint for audiovisual equipment, CDs and videos, will diminish the impact of technology on an interior. Antique wardrobes provide excellent storage options because they are deep enough to accommodate televisions and hi-fi equipment, new shelving can be inserted for maximum efficiency and they add an ancient feature in contrast to, or connection with, other elements.

When you put anything into an area always work with prominent architectural features like a ceiling rose, wooden panelling, a central motif on the floor, or an obvious symmetry in the position of doors or the alignment of windows. Disjunctions and asymmetry create visual tensions that can have a negative impact. For example, placing an armoire off-centre against the wall between two French windows in a period house highlights a fine piece of furniture but also draws attention to the fact that it is off-centre. Placing it in the middle of the wall creates a sense of harmony between the different elements – the windows and the armoire – and in the arrangement as a whole.

LEFT Different functions within this open-plan living area progress logically from cooking to dining to relaxing. The contrast between a contemporary modular sofa and an antique table reinforces a sense of division.
ABOVE This understairs area is an unusual yet appealing setting for a long, low bench. Felt pads, sheepskin rugs and cushions made with Moroccan fabrics add essential comfort.

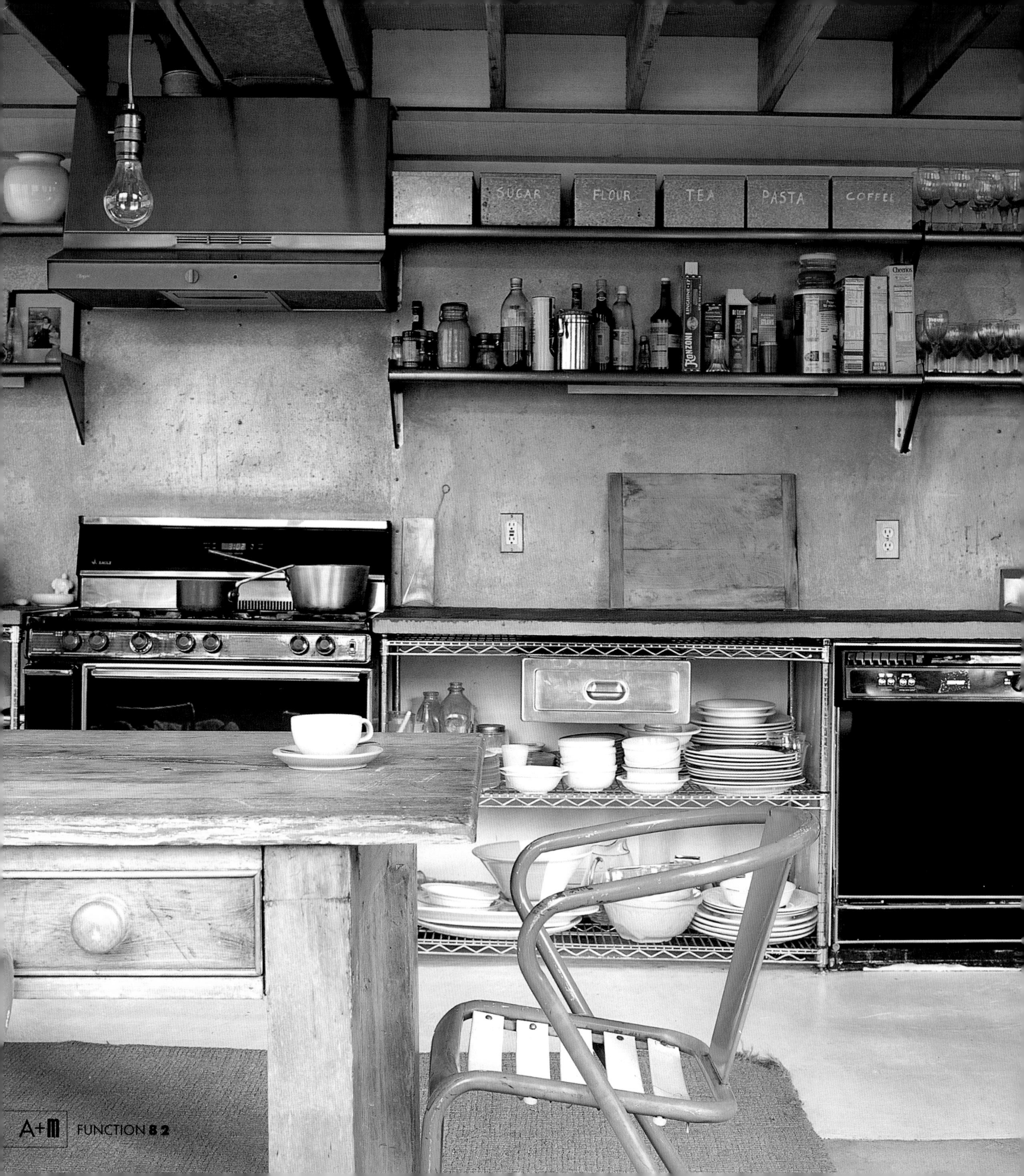
SUGAR
FLOUR
TEA
PASTA
COFFEE

Cooking and eating

In many homes today the kitchen area is a centre where people meet to cook, eat and relax, so what it looks like and how it contributes to the atmosphere of your home is as important as its efficiency. The main considerations when designing a kitchen area are whether to choose freestanding or fitted units and furniture, or a mixture, and whether the space will function purely as a kitchen or be used for other activities. Flooring, walls, work surfaces and storage all provide the potential to combine ancient and modern, either in relation to the structure of the building – a modern stainless-steel kitchen in a period house, for example – or by mixing old and new elements like an antique cupboard, salvage taps, a butler's sink and a contemporary worktop.

THIS PAGE Industrial stainless-steel fittings and appliances combine with Japanese-style elements, including a traditional storage cupboard, drawer units, shoji screens, paper lantern and slate floor, to create a precise and orderly kitchen area. **OPPOSITE** Organized along a single wall, freestanding stainless-steel fittings, a blue stone worktop and a professional-size cooker are compatible with the raw industrial structure of a former brick factory. The pine country table and natural-coloured rug add textural contrast.

Select and work with materials, colours and finishes that are in keeping with the style of kitchen you want. Hard-edge materials such as concrete, metal and glass are suitable for an industrial style, whereas natural ones like wood, stone and slate are suited to a country-style kitchen. Use contemporary, salvage or ancient materials as appropriate or combine different materials to create a variety of styles and effects. For example, you could insert a piece of marble from an old dairy between sections of new wood, or lay old tiles and cover them with glass to provide a sealed work surface. Give all old surfaces a professional clean and reseal wood with tung oil to make it water-repellent and protect it against staining. However, it may be difficult to remove all stains – and smells – from old wood and stone.

Keep the design and overall concept simple, functional and easy to clean and maintain. Practicality, safety and ease of use are paramount in a kitchen area. The minimum requirement is a core of permanent work surfaces, cooking equipment and storage units: a simple arrangement of appliances and fitted units with a hard-wearing worktop, possibly along one wall or in a central block to define and contain the kitchen area, provides all the essential basics.

Painting fitted units and shelving the same colour as the walls and investing in a good-quality work surface, possibly made from recycled wood or slate, is cost-efficient and avoids the anonymity of flat-pack designs. This will also create a harmonious contrast to a feature element such as a Victorian plate rack or an old glass-and-metal display cabinet for storing glassware or herbs. Depending on your budget, you can elaborate on the basics, for example by installing high-specification industrial equipment such as stainless-steel shelving for storing pans and heavy cookware.

LEFT In view from the whole space, well-chosen elements and a free-standing cooker provide a multifunction, low-key kitchen area in a loft. The home-made high-level table is both a convenient work surface and an alternative place to sit and eat. A section of wall by the door, a useful device for containing storage shelves, and a change in flooring are reminders of the loft's original division of space. OPPOSITE The former sitting room of a nineteenth-century country house is now a general family area for cooking, eating and relaxing, with a long pine table and colourful Arne Jacobsen chairs. Installing kitchen appliances and fittings in parallel blocks behind a low wall ensures the whole area works on all levels. Overspill storage in a separate pantry and a laundry area through the door on the left facilitate this low-key arrangement.

For appliances, it is generally best to choose modern products. Although traditional enamel cookers work well in an eclectic arrangement of elements they are in high demand and short supply. Finding and possibly reconditioning a second-hand traditional American fridge can take many weeks. Instead, check out appliances for commercial kitchens, for example oversized designs in heavy-duty materials such as steel and reinforced glass. An alternative is to buy standard appliances and combine function and aesthetics by concealing them with fascia panels or by housing them creatively – for example, slot a cooker into a line of freestanding, low-level, country-style cupboard and drawer units and cover the units with a stainless-steel, marble or slate worktop. (Fix metal panels to any wood surfaces adjacent to the sides of the cooker to prevent the risk of fire.) Or install a fridge in an antique cupboard or wardrobe.

(Remove the cupboard base for stability, and check the doors of the cupboard and fridge align. If they don't, remove the lower section of the doorframe for access.) Alternatively, slot the fridge into a purpose-built box with an optional door. The box can be made from salvage tongue-and-grooving or sheets of copper or steel on a plywood frame.

If your kitchen is also an eating area choose a table and chairs for their aesthetic appeal, and the colour, shape and texture they add to an ancient and modern environment, as well as for their efficiency. In a contemporary all-white kitchen area, for example, an antique table with aluminium chairs is an inviting place to sit; or combine a rosewood table with translucent plastic chairs. Keep to a core group of textures and materials to create a harmonious arrangement and introduce single blocks of enlivening colours and textures, for example a modern table with a colourful laminate surface in contrast to old floorboards.

Whether a dining table and chairs are part of a kitchen, a general living ar
elements that work within the overall environment and all

The modest structure of
this wooden beach house,
built in the 1920s, sets a
standard of practical
simplicity for decoration and
furniture. Painted walls and
floors in bright new colours
update the structure of the
space and the scrubbed
bare-top painted table and
junk-shop country chairs
combine to create an easy-
to-maintain kitchen and
dining area.

The imposing structure of
this sixteenth-century
farmhouse, with stone
floors, bare plaster walls
and a walk-in fireplace,
requires furniture of a
similar scale to balance the
proportions and architectural
style of the room. The
circular table, made from a
piece of plywood set on
wooden blocks, was cut to
fit the space.

r in a separate room, aim to create a welcoming combination of elaxed and pleasurable dining.

In this open-plan New York loft, with painted walls and polished floorboards throughout, the challenge was to create a focus for different activities without compromising a sense of integration. Parallel shelving with a display of collectable glass is a simple and effective way of defining the dining area, which has a home-made table and contemporary aluminium chairs.

This intimate dining alcove within a vast New York loft provides ample opportunity for juxtapositions between ancient and modern architecture and elements. The matt surfaces of an ancient wooden Indian table, plain chairs and elegantly simple copper lamps contrast with the high-gloss painted panelling, black wooden floors and a magnificent window.

THIS PAGE This linen-tented, wooden four-poster bed provides enclosure and privacy in contrast to the sense of space, light and openness in a London loft. Linen curtains, a fake fur throw and a kilim counterbalance the hard-edged architecture.
OPPOSITE An artful arrangement of an antique wardrobe, bed frame and standard-lamp base in a New York bedroom is given an inexpensive update with a simple injection of colour. The pink mohair blanket adds warmth and vibrancy.

Sleeping

A good night's sleep is vital to our physical, mental and emotional well-being. Creating the best possible environment for this within an ancient and modern space means balancing a high level of comfort, for example from a good-quality mattress, with well-chosen furniture, textiles, lighting and objects from the past. The combination can be as direct as a rustic nineteenth-century Indian bed in a pared-down room or a romantic antique Spanish chandelier in an otherwise modern interior. Too much visual stimulation or too many pieces of furniture can conflict with the area's main function, so limit the elements to essentials to promote rest and relaxation.

A bed can be an ornamental decorative feature or a simple base and mattress with colour and texture provided by the bedlinen. A contemporary futon standing on rush-covered tatami mats and covered with an antique silk quilt can be as inviting and beautiful as an antique four-poster with crisp linens and plaid blankets. Consider a bed in the context of its surroundings and give it space and definition regardless of its worth.

Period beds normally have substantial frames that isolate them from other elements in a space, making them the focal point. An antique French bed with ornate wooden carving, a simple Victorian dormitory bed with an iron frame or an eighteenth-century four-poster would be a distinctive centrepiece in any ancient and modern environment. For maximum contrast install it in a contemporary space, or in a period home offset it against a wall with a single block of colour, wooden boarding or uneven plaster.

If a bed is to be part of an ensemble of ancient and modern pieces, try to balance it with another item. For example a contemporary metal bed could be balanced by an Indian wardrobe. Also, position elements to create a sense of symmetry, such as by placing a pair of modern reading lamps on either side of an antique bed; add a large rug for contrast and definition.

Clutter-free is stress-free, so provide ample storage for clothing and belongings. A combination of hanging space and drawers or shelving can accommodate all the basics. This can be an inexpensive option like a row of traditional peg hooks with various sizes of woven baskets underneath for T-shirts, jeans and socks; or a more costly one such as an extensive Shaker-style wall of built-in drawers and cupboards. Alternatively, install an architectural feature and conceal storage behind a low partition wall or a series of floor-to-ceiling sliding panels.

All the care and planning that goes into creating a welcoming and soothing sleeping area means it can become an overspill or alternative space for general relaxation. A bed can be an ideal setting for reading, a relaxing massage, listening to music or, if you have children, playing. It is important to choose and position one so that it will accommodate all its uses and users. To vary light levels and alter the atmosphere, fit a dimmer switch to a central ambient light, for example a glass pendant or Japanese paper lantern. An anglepoise or other directional lamp on a bedside table or on the floor next to your bed is necessary for reading, and can be turned upwards as an uplighter.

THIS PAGE, FROM TOP
Positioning this simple bed base and mattress to line up below a prominent roof apex makes the bed central and important to the area as well as promoting a sense of order and symmetry.
In this pared-down historic country house, luxury bedside lighting combines with basic inexpensive elements and a colourful blanket to create a comfortable and welcoming bedroom.
The difference in scale between this contemporary, hospital-style bed and the high ceilings in a nineteenth-century house creates an enchanting Alice-in-Wonderland illusion. The contrast between the scale of the prints and the standard-sized door compounds the effect.
A confident mix of raw brickwork, gentleman's-club-style panelling and ancient Indian doors creates a bold and exotic environment for an oversized bed with silk bolster and valance.

In spite of the industrial plastic pleating installed to provide optional separation, the antique Indian bed and bedlinen create a romantic sleeping area. Orientating the bed away from the window optimizes the sense of connection in an open-plan space.

Antique baths like this zinc one with a
fake wood surround – or even a
commonplace Victorian roll-top bath
with ball-and-claw feet – look good, so it
is worth making them a central feature
in an ancient and modern space. Fitting
a lavatory and shower in separate
compartments in this Paris apartment
keeps the contrasts between elements
and architecture direct and simple.

Bathing

Showering or bathing is a daily necessity as well as an opportunity to soothe tension and revitalize your body. The success of a bathing area depends on a good supply of hot water and effective water pressure, ventilation and heating. The efficiency of modern pumps and thermostats in providing this essential – and usually invisible – backup for appliances means that it is possible to experience a back-pummelling performance shower even with an antique shower fitting.

The patina and shapes of baths, basins, fixtures and fittings – ancient or modern – make strong visual statements within a space. A Victorian roll-top bath in front of a wall of glass bricks in a loft is an example. Alternatively, combine ancient and modern fittings and details: an antique zinc bath with a contemporary glass basin and a mono-block tap, or standard modern bathroom furniture offset with antique mirrors. In this way clinical efficiency can be balanced with aesthetics and worn textures.

Floor-to-ceiling and wall-to-wall tiling is effective waterproofing but painted plaster or wood can be given adequate protection by applying a gloss glaze. Combining tiling with another material is an opportunity to introduce contrasts. In a Japanese-style bathing area slate tiles on the walls, floor and around the bathtub are offset by paper-and-wood sliding shoji screens.

How a bathing area relates to the rest of a space, for example whether or not it interconnects with a sleeping area, requires consideration and planning. While some areas suggest a perfect setting for a bath or shower – under a sloping roof, in front of a grand fireplace or in the bay window of a sleeping area – it is important to check with a plumber before you progress with any schemes. Installing or moving water pipes, soil pipes and drains is expensive and disruptive so the cost-efficient option is often to optimize what exists.

Consider how much privacy you need to feel comfortable. In a loft-style apartment in London, positioning an antique roll-top so that it can be seen from every part of the open-plan environment gives the space a sense of freedom and integration. However, before you take down walls to create openness consider the privacy factor from all angles – including from the outside looking in. If you are concerned about interruption by people you live with, a division of some kind is essential. Even if you live on your own, bathing is sometimes more relaxing in an enclosure of some kind. Translucent sliding panels in Perspex or glass, shoji screens, low-budget hospital screens (available from professional equipment suppliers) or inexpensive shower curtains all provide a degree of separation without blocking light.

Install suitable low-level or adjustable ambient lighting for relaxing in the bath, with task lighting beside a mirror. Bathroom lighting must conform with national safety regulations so if you want to install antique lights have them checked by an expert.

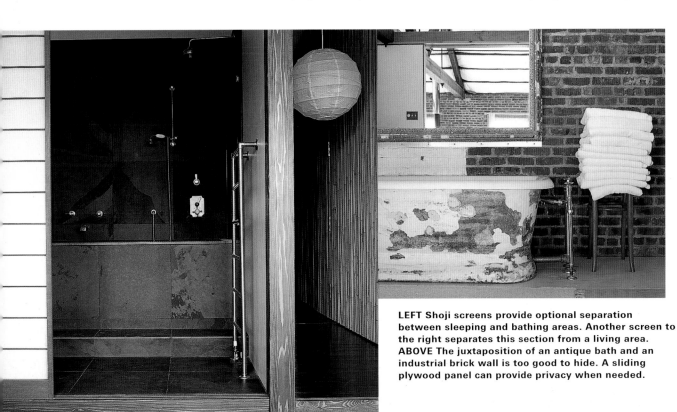

LEFT Shoji screens provide optional separation between sleeping and bathing areas. Another screen to the right separates this section from a living area. ABOVE The juxtaposition of an antique bath and an industrial brick wall is too good to hide. A sliding plywood panel can provide privacy when needed.

Working

Planning an area to work in means assessing how important the activity is to you and how much time you spend on it, then deciding on the equipment you need. This will determine the amount of space required. Running a business from home is not the same as sitting down to pay bills or process a weekly grocery shop online. Each requires a very different setup and commitment of resources and space, and presents very different options for ancient and modern combinations.

If you work from home it is worth committing a separate space as a work area, with specialist furniture and lighting, a phone, computer equipment and other technology. The advantages are that it will provide privacy and quiet, and you won't disturb others while you work. You will also be able to consider its style and arrangement in its own right rather than in relation to another area – and if space is not at a premium you will be less likely to underestimate your needs.

Finding the right desk for your computer – and the right chair to go with it – is essential. As it can be difficult to source an antique desk with a worktop that is the right height and depth for using a keyboard it may be preferable to use a custom-built computer desk or trolley and offset this with ancient furniture and details such as a wooden or metal filing cabinet, or an antique kilim underfoot, to add texture, colour and individuality.

If you set up a work area as part of a dual-function space try to ensure it receives adequate light and fresh air – or use mobile furniture for easy cross-overs between different activities. Consider the position of a computer screen and avoid the glare of a back-lit screen or reflections of light on a screen. If necessary, modulate incoming light with blinds.

Work furniture and equipment are not easy to camouflage so avoid using part of a living area as a home office unless you plan to conceal it in some way. Divisions such as contemporary sliding panels or salvaged folding doors, possibly across a section of the relaxing area, will provide efficient screening.

Creating a small-scale work area for projects like household management or dealing with personal finances is a good idea as these activities do not logically integrate with any others. A desk with drawers or compartments is useful for filing documents. Choose and position it to integrate with the overall scheme of the space.

ABOVE A mid-twentieth-century anglepoise lamp makes an effective contrast with an elegant rosewood desk. Antique desks add character to home offices but custom-made contemporary desks are preferable for long spells of computer work. **BELOW LEFT** Placing this Arts and Crafts desk and chair next to a window creates a light and appealing work area.

THIS PAGE This flip-down antique desk looks like a chest of drawers but it contains a comprehensive system of compartments and drawers – ideal as a part-time worktable for processing household bills and correspondence.
OPPOSITE BELOW RIGHT Plastic screens pinned to a timber beam blur the visual impact of a professional office and provide important separation in a family space.

A+m

Loft conversion

ANCIENT ORIENTAL LIVING IN A CONTEMPORARY OPEN-PLAN SPACE

A loft-style apartment on London's South Bank is a large open-plan space with flexible divisions between different areas, along the lines of a traditional Japanese interior. It was originally three apartments, two with spectacular views and a third at the back of the building. The conversion, by architects Ushida Findlay, combines the positive aspects of all three spaces with a bold mix of natural materials in an imaginative adaptation of oriental living.

The apartment is now an inverted L-shape, the base of which is a wide space with a wall of windows and glass. This incorporates two of the three original apartments and has stunning views of Tate Modern, the Thames and the city skyline. Formal arrangements of a traditional long,

MAIN PICTURE The orientation of the main living area takes full advantage of a magnificent view. Traditional Chinese furniture and a curving wall of bamboo add colour, shape and enlivening juxtapositions.
LEFT As views are such a big feature of the space, many elements are orientated towards windows, like this chair and footstool, which are positioned for quiet contemplation.

low table, sofa, armchairs and a high-back chair and footstool orientate this area towards the view. Antique Chinese cupboards provide storage for entertainment equipment and books.

A curving bamboo wall sweeping down the length of the apartment connects the front and back areas – incorporating the third original apartment – and emphasizes their different functions. The front of the space is a social public area, while the back is private. The bamboo wall also conceals storage for housewares, clothes and books.

The main entrance to the apartment is a bamboo-covered door midway along the bamboo wall. Opposite this is a wide opening made from stained wooden beams, which looks like an oriental rugby goal, with a wooden crossbeam extending on each side to connect with, and form part of, a kitchen to the left and a tatami room on the right.

In Japan space is measured by the number of tatami mats – mats made from straw and covered in rushes – that fit into it. The dimensions of the tatami room are based on this precise method of measurement. The basic structural element in the space, a wooden base and frame that slot together without nails, was made in Japan, then dismantled and shipped to the site. Traditional shoji screens – wooden frames with paper infills – slide in the frame to conceal or reveal the area within. Tatami mats provide a soft, textural base for low-level living, and there is an antique low table for traditional Japanese dining. The area is also used for relaxing and as an alternative sleeping space; futons are stored in a built-in cupboard in the room.

The appreciation of natural materials and the Japanese influence throughout the loft extend to riven slate floor tiles, an authentic textured render on the walls in the main living area, and textured Japanese wallpaper in the tatami room. This influence is also evident in the use of lanterns to draw attention to different areas in the space.

The kitchen area next to the tatami room is less purist, although no less ingenious. Traditional redwood cupboards contain standard kitchen equipment and the room incorporates an authentic cabinet for storage. Shoji screens divide the kitchen from the rest of the space, or slide open to offer views into the tatami room.

The bamboo corridor starts as a wide opening alongside the sitting area, narrows as it passes the kitchen and the tatami room, and continues towards the main sleeping and bathing areas at the back of the apartment. This is the private part of the space; a shoji screen across the opening allows it to be closed off from the rest of the apartment.

Whereas the bamboo wall is simply inspired by oriental style, the tatami room and shoji screens are imaginative installations of traditional Japanese design elements. They work well in the scale of the space and are a brilliant solution for dividing the loft into different areas without blocking light or compromising a sense of openness and connection.

BELOW The curving lines of the chair and the comfort of the antique footstool, positioned near a textured plaster wall, create a welcoming individual seating area.
RIGHT The bamboo wall runs the entire length of the apartment, connecting every area within the space. It also provides extensive hidden storage.

Made to precise Japanese measurements, the tatami room, complete with traditional sliding shoji screens and natural soft matting, provides the option of an enclosure within this open-plan space for dining, relaxing or sleeping.

Interior architecture

CONTEMPORARY MINIMALISM IN A NINETEENTH-CENTURY NEW YORK TOWN HOUSE

An ornate marble fire surround is a striking original feature in the main living area of this pared-down space and influences the formal arrangement of furniture. The shapes of a low table – a slice of a tree trunk with bark on both sides yet planed to a smooth finish on top – and flowering plants add organic forms without deviating from a powerful orderly scheme.

In this apartment in a Manhattan town house nothing is left of the nineteenth-century configuration of space or architectural detailing, apart from a marble fire surround and sash windows at the front of the building. As architect Stephen Roberts demonstrates with this precision-engineering style of architecture, it is possible to combine an ancient building with rigorous minimalist reduction without sacrificing a perfect finish.

The apartment has its own entrance and extends the full length and width of the original town house, from the sash windows in the front to a courtyard garden at the back, which is entered through modern metal-frame French windows. Although the interior has been reinvented to create a purist contemporary environment, the space progresses in a conventional line from a formal sitting area to a kitchen area, a dining area and finally to sleeping and bathing areas. The simple logic of this progression strengthens the scheme.

It removes any conflict between the original design and layout of the space and how it works today, and focuses energy and attention on the overall sense of space, light, shape and colour.

Starting with the hallway and the view ahead into the work area – a tall, slim slot of space that runs half the length of the apartment behind the sitting and dining areas and has a built-in worktable – it is apparent that this project is about taking control and not deviating from a plan because of an original lack of precision, misalignment or architectural detail.

Every area is at once spartan and impressive in its simplicity, finish and sense of order and space. Yet there is no lack of shape or texture. The more you look, the more you see. The main living area is an ideal example. Two identical off-white Paolo Lenti sofas in felt upholstery face each other across a low table made from a section of a tree trunk; the bark on the sides contrasts with the smoothness of the wood. A Charlotte Perriand bookcase from around 1920, without books, and white low-level cabinets with lacquered metal doors suspended along one wall, add shape and practical storage. The cupboards hold objects like candlesticks and bowls that are not always in use. Apart from colourful Plexiglas rods, which stand above the fireplace or on the floor by the window to reflect light, the area is without colour or decoration.

A floor-to-ceiling opening connects with the rest of the space and leads past a slim kitchen to the dining area. The kitchen consists of two identical low-level blocks of units, parallel to each other like the sofas, with built-in appliances and stainless-steel worktops. Everything is put away. To make a cup of tea it is necessary to take out a kettle, tea bag and cup. Brilliant storage and planning make this a simple undertaking.

The dining area is the plainest in the apartment with a horizontal light above a classic Knoll table and chairs. Benches provide alternative seating. Any pieces of furniture that are not in use are kept in the work area, which is accessible through a doorway in the wall behind the table. Beyond the dining area is a raw-timber bed designed by the owners.

The front and back windows are the main sources of daylight, apart from two slim ones with sandblasted glass in the middle of one side of the apartment. Consequently, it was important to allow light to reach the centre of the space. Folding glass-and-metal doors provide optional separation between the dining and sleeping areas. The glass is opaque to provide privacy without blocking light. With light behind them, the doors glow a pale green. Wraparound white ceilings, walls and poured terrazzo floors add to the clean, pure aesthetic of the space and to the sense of light.

Furniture and objects, including a Georges Jouve vase from the 1950s, are kept to a minimum. This is typical of the pure aesthetic of the apartment. Simply reducing it to a series of finely planned areas with extensive storage liberates the space from excessive furniture and detail so that a simple bed, or a table with benches, fulfils all requirements. It is a triumph of the overall scheme that such diverse elements as a heritage fireplace from the nineteenth century and a contemporary raw-timber table work so well together.

BELOW Although the apartment is open-plan, each area is contained and partly separated by the architecture without any loss of integration. This arrangement is supported by furniture that focuses on one activity, for example a vintage Knoll table and chairs in the dining area.
RIGHT A narrow kitchen, which slots in between the sitting and dining areas, consists of two parallel blocks of cupboards with stainless-steel worktops. One counter is a seamless plane; the other contains a hob and two sinks. The kettle is from a New York flea market.

ABOVE The apartment extends the full length of a basement area. This view, from the bedroom at the back, looks towards the sitting area at the front of the house. Glass doors provide optional separation without blocking light from the central core of the space. **LEFT** Display is selective within this minimal white space yet it introduces vital contrasting colour, shape and form. In the sitting area, a sculpture by Vasa sits on the floor by an original window or on the mantel shelf. Ceramics by Georges Jouve in the kitchen and dining areas complete the art list. The insides of the shutters are plain – without architraving – in keeping with the minimal interior. The box beneath the window conceals a cast-iron radiator.

ELEMENTS

'Have nothing in your house that you do not know to be useful and believe to be beautiful.' William Morris

THIS PAGE An inherited dresser is the centrepiece of this eclectic mix of furniture, textiles and artefacts, which includes Liberty chairs, a modern oval table and a graphic banner made from an African kuba cloth. PREVIOUS PAGES The worn surfaces of a painted wooden chest of drawers and a plaster wall connect and reduce the impact of their intense colours. The random brushwork on the wall offsets the fine markings on a contemporary ceramic by Rupert Spira.

Whether you are putting together a capsule collection of essential furniture, reviewing what you already have or looking for a specific piece, the way the elements are combined is central to the success of an ancient and modern space.

There are many variations on how old and new items of furniture can be used in an interior. Juxtapose modern pieces with an ancient architectural feature or add antique furniture to a modern space. Group old and new items to create contrast – contemporary aluminium chairs with an old oak dining table, for example – or use the texture and colour of an upholstery fabric to link a sofa with armchairs from a different period.

If you are mixing ancient and modern items from diverse cultures or styles, stick to predominantly simple shapes and pieces that are made from one material such as wood or metal, or upholstered in one fabric. An example is a collection of antique wooden chairs contrasted with a contemporary metal table, or an eclectic mix of an old country wooden chair, a contemporary plastic chair and a contemporary metal chair with an antique country table. It is easier to combine elements that are not combinations in themselves. To this simple and well-defined mix it is then possible to add a decorative item without undermining an overall sense of harmony. For example, a decorative metal-and-glass low table could be combined with a group of second-hand armchairs re-covered in grey linen.

If you inherited your furniture, or if it has accumulated over the years, fitting it into an ancient and modern space may present a challenge. Deciding which pieces to keep, which can be modified, and which may need to be removed comes down to personal preference. Looking beyond the furniture to the structure of a space, for example the colour of the walls or flooring, can suggest how to create an ancient and modern environment using existing pieces. If you love a particular item, or it is important to you as a family heirloom, make this a centrepiece or a starting point when you review the possibilities.

This chapter explores a wide range of options for using sofas, tables, chairs and storage furniture to enrich an ancient and modern space while fulfilling the practical needs of a contemporary home.

Furniture for relaxing

Furniture that encourages relaxation is an essential element in a living space, whether you prefer a traditional cushioned sofa upholstered in suede or antique kilims, a French nineteenth-century wrought-iron daybed with a calico mattress or a mid-twentieth-century iconic armchair. Depending on the arrangement you want – an informal group of antique armchairs and a linear modern sofa, for example, or an eclectic mix of nineteenth-century armchairs in a modern apartment – ancient furniture offers great potential for enlivening combinations. Reupholstering a sofa or armchair, or making a loose cover for it, provides an opportunity to totally reinvent it. A Victorian chesterfield that looks pretty and unremarkable in chintz becomes a very different piece of furniture if it is upholstered in grey mohair. Or leave worn, even threadbare, antique upholstery like damask or tapestry in its original state for contrast and a sense of history in a contemporary environment.

A mix of antique fabrics and the patina of antique frames will connect very different styles and periods of furniture, whether the frames are wood, wicker, bamboo or cast iron. For example, in a New York loft a baroque dark wood bench-style sofa with a velvet seat cushion, a Victorian parlour sofa in flock velvet and faux bamboo armchairs with silk seat covers coexist in artful harmony.

The colours and textures of antique fabrics work well with modern structural treatments like bare floorboards or plain brick, stone or plaster walls. Or, for a harmonious combination of ancient furniture with a contemporary space, re-cover the pieces in an unobtrusive fabric like ticking or felt. Reupholstering individual pieces in the same colour but different fabrics – cream wool, linen and cotton, for example – or in the same fabric in a family of colours – linen in shades of yellow and ochre – will unify even eccentric items.

Antique sofas and chairs may require rebuilding or padding before they are reupholstered. This is expensive and can change a pleasingly misshapen piece into a plain one. If you buy furniture from a dealer ask for advice on this, and if you plan to repair an original fabric check with an upholsterer. Loose covers are a good way to unify or simplify elements without detracting from their original state.

Contemporary sofas and chairs, with their lightweight frames, linear designs and high-specification stretchy, stain-resistant or blended fabrics in a good range of colours add comfort and pace to an ancient and modern interior. In a converted English cow shed with stone walls and flagstone floors an electric-blue foam-based sofa with a metal frame provides a single seating option. It is as practical as it is dynamic – in summer children sit on it with wet swimsuits. Modular seating is flexible – it can be split into individual seats or put together along a wall in an industrial loft conversion or into the corner of a cottage.

The effect a contemporary piece has on an interior can be very different to that of an ancient one. For example, the simplicity of line and construction of a Terence Woodgate sofa draws attention to the objects around it. This is not a caution against contemporary design but an affirmation of it. Any piece that sparks a review of the other elements in a space is a positive addition as it can result in a more pared-down, harmonious interior. If introducing a contemporary design makes other furniture look out of place, edit your existing pieces, ancient and modern, and review the overall space. Adding a rug or changing a wall colour, for example, can provide a vital link between ancient and modern elements.

THIS PAGE The way the velvet has softened and faded on this old chesterfield is part of the sofa's appeal. Pragmatic mismatching repairs add to its idiosyncratic form.

OPPOSITE, FROM TOP

The classic club aesthetic in this New York loft includes shining wooden floors, chrome anglepoise lamps, zebra skins and traditional worn leather armchairs. The Antony chair by Jean Prouvé, like many iconic mid-twentieth-century chairs in demand for contemporary homes, was originally designed for commercial use.

Different shades and textures of white connect an expansive tweedy sofa, originally designed by Florence Knoll in 1954, a contemporary paper lantern and nineteenth-century wooden panelling in this Paris apartment.

The shape and form of this modern Swedish chair in metal, wood and leather provides comfort in an open-plan area without blocking light and views across the space or access to the garden.

THIS PAGE Using black vinyl to re-cover the seat pads on a set of ordinary plywood café chairs updates and upgrades them.
OPPOSITE LEFT A Knoll table and a set of classic Knoll chairs with woven leather seats and backs add warmth and texture to a pared-down contemporary setting.
OPPOSITE CENTRE The curving backs of these Eames chairs contrast with the strong lines of nineteenth-century panelling, recycled floorboards and a contemporary table.
OPPOSITE RIGHT The worn texture and irregular shape of these benches, found in the street, contrast with the straight lines and hard surfaces of an Art Deco apartment.

Practical chairs and tables

Hardbacked chairs, benches and tables are versatile items. They are mainly used for dining areas but can be utilized throughout a space. For example, a circular pine Victorian table and a contemporary bentwood chair placed by a window make a welcoming reading area. A contemporary glass-top and metal-frame table is useful for storage and display in a bedroom, an old wooden refectory bench is ideal for a hall, and a wooden chair of any period provides a warm dressing chair in a bathroom.

Unlike soft furniture, these practical items are difficult to modify. Whereas it is possible to diminish the grandeur of an eighteenth-century baroque armchair or elevate a Victorian parlour sofa with upholstery, a hardbacked dining or occasional chair is what it is. A neoclassical walnut one is redolent of bygone wealth and status. A rustic or ethnic chair, simply constructed from natural materials, retains a sense of the resourcefulness of the time when it was made. Painting it simply changes its colour.

However, the context in which these practical items are used changes the way they are perceived. In a pared-down modern environment the simplest ancient dark-wood chair will take on a powerful silhouette, while the elegant simplicity of a bentwood, Shaker ladderback or African ironwood chair will add contrast and character to an area of soft seating, as well as providing an alternative place to sit. In Gert van de Keuken's Art Deco apartment in Paris pieces of furniture found in the street – an old wooden workbench and a pair of elongated low benches – are the focus of the dining area.

As well as old chairs intended for use in the home, there are many practical and inexpensive alternatives designed for church halls, schools and community centres that transfer easily into an ancient and modern environment. The workaday integrity of these items makes them ideal for functional spaces such as kitchen dining areas and family bathrooms. Some of these chairs do not always align comfortably with dining tables so check the height of the seats before you buy eight of them for your dining area. Bentwood or bamboo chairs with open backs are useful if space is at a premium as light will pass through them and they do not block views across an interior.

Chairs with high seats come into their own in a kitchen, next to a worktable or worktop. Office or dressmaker's chairs, and stools with a swivel base and adjustable heights, are infinitely useful, sculptural designs.

If a table is to be used for dining it is important to choose one – ancient or modern – that is the right size and shape for the space and that complements, or contrasts with, the other elements. In a pared-down environment a dining table offers an opportunity to make a bold ancient and modern statement. For example, in a period house with plain walls and stripped floors a primitive worm-eaten oak country table could be juxtaposed with a contemporary chandelier and aluminium chairs.

If you live in a compact space but like to invite friends for supper, an extendable table is a flexible solution. Options include an antique rosewood circular table with flip-up sides – one side can be kept up for regular use and the dining area can be enlarged when required.

It is also possible to adapt a table intended for a particular purpose to another, quite different, use. For example, a former school worktable can be converted into a dining table by cutting down the legs and re-covering the top with a thin flexible sheet of copper, which can be lightly hammered or pinned to fit around the edges.

In a pared-down eighteenth-century sitting room, this wooden country table and chairs – bought at a flea market – provide an alternative seating area to a kitchen-dining space in the basement. A simple black plastic cover on the table contrasts with the white walls and ceiling, and reflects light from a Georgian sash window. The patina on the chairs and table legs connects with the original wooden floor.

This light and spacious New York loft is a harmonious mix of flea-market finds, elegant handmade furniture, such as this simple dining/work table, and a few contemporary pieces to update the overall look. Although they were made decades apart, these chairs are remarkably similar in design.

within a contemporary environment is more effective than a jumble or scattering of pieces. elements and the structure of the space bold and obvious.

Handmade in 1937 for a nearby village hall, this monumental table occupies one part of a vast studio in a former church. The wavy lines of the thick table top, and the simple flowing outline and lightness of the Arne Jacobsen chairs, make a dynamic ancient and modern combination.

In a pared-down cooking and eating area with white-painted walls, bare stripped floorboards and clinical-style stainless-steel wall units, a Victorian jeweller's table looks like a contemporary sculpture. Used in isolation in this way, a carefully chosen item of antique furniture acquires definition and a powerful presence.

Occasional tables and stools

Combining practicality and aesthetic appeal, and working in support of larger items of furniture, occasional and low-level tables and stools help to create comfort and individuality in an ancient and modern space.

Occasional tables in sitting areas provide surfaces for books, lamps and artefacts, and somewhere to sit and read a paper or eat lunch. In an ancient environment contemporary glass-top or metal tables add a pool of reflection and light and produce a bold juxtaposition. If you are using two different tables in the same area, perhaps a low one for books and magazines and a console table for art displays, mix shapes and textures and even periods of design for variety and contrast. In furniture-maker Andrew Mortada's conversion of an artisan's studio in London an Arts and Crafts console table with a display of African pots, baskets and carvings is juxtaposed with a contemporary oval table with cast-concrete legs and a stone-effect top. The pared-down brick, glass and concrete of the surroundings underline and unite the very different shape and construction of each table.

Low-level tables are primarily for storing books and magazines, and displaying decorative items like an ethnic bowl for fruit. If you have a collection of remote controls for entertainment equipment, keeping them together on a low table in a contemporary glass dish or an African basket combines practical organization with an appealing decorative object. If you want to enliven a space with accent lighting on low-level tables, use contemporary glass or plastic globes to conceal bare bulbs.

Low-level stools provide indispensable supplementary seating and are useful surfaces on which to put a plate of food, a drink, a book or your feet. From ancient African milking stools to Philippe Starck's colourful plastic Bubu or Prince Aha stools, these items enliven, and add flexibility to, an ancient and modern interior.

CLOCKWISE FROM OPPOSITE TOP LEFT
A stool with woven string or raffia across a wooden frame is a common junk-shop find. Use it as a low table or stool and store it under a larger table or seat when not in use.
Designed for milking goats this low African stool is a challenging place to sit, especially for long periods. However, it is an appealing sculptural piece for a contemporary space. The fine construction and finish of this low table or stool is typical of traditional oriental crafts. Pieces like these are inexpensive and make ideal footstools for use with a sofa or hardbacked chair.
The natural texture of raffia suggests waterside living, so this cotton-reel stool is perfect in a Long Island beach house.
Juxtaposed with a contemporary lamp and art, an ordinary table is transformed into the focus of a simple bedroom.
This long bench is used for displaying new work in ceramicist Rupert Spira's studio. The dark, worn ancient wood makes a bold contrast with lime-washed floorboards.
This mid-twentieth-century two-tier table is practical as well as decorative. Magazines and remote controls can be stored out of sight, leaving the top as a plain shape or a surface for display.

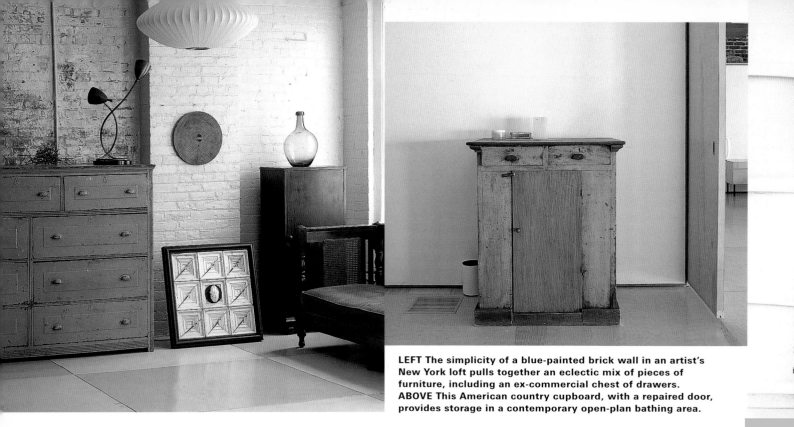

LEFT The simplicity of a blue-painted brick wall in an artist's New York loft pulls together an eclectic mix of pieces of furniture, including an ex-commercial chest of drawers. **ABOVE** This American country cupboard, with a repaired door, provides storage in a contemporary open-plan bathing area.

Storage

Storage is a key factor in creating an ancient and modern environment that is enjoyable and comfortable to live in. With adequate storage, which can be either built-in or freestanding or a mixture of both, the architectural elements become clearly visible, without the distraction of everyday clutter. Freestanding pieces like cupboards, chests and wardrobes are features in their own right and can be used to create exciting contrasts with walls and floors.

Finding a balance between what to reveal or conceal, and deciding on the kind of storage you want, depends on the amount of space you require. Clothes, housewares and appliances can be hidden in built-in storage that looks like a structural feature – a curving sculptural wall, for example, with access from either side, or a series of sliding panels that conceal a section of storage space. Architectural solutions like these, which contrast, or fuse, with the original structure work well with different styles of architecture.

Period storage pieces in bold shapes and colours can be especially effective in an ancient and modern environment: an ornate French armoire for china and glass in a kitchen area, for example, or a red lacquer oriental chest for storing bedlinen in a modern bedroom. If you want to use such a feature it is worth providing built-in storage as a backup – over-filling a rustic dresser with china and glassware or piling books and magazines on an eighteenth-century chest of drawers will diminish the impact of the piece.

Country-style furniture, junk-shop finds and antiques can provide imaginative storage options. Examples include a food safe with a wooden frame and punched tin panels and shelves, for a television cabinet; an old baker's trolley with slatted wooden shelves bleached from years of use, for books or clothing; and an antique wooden chest of drawers as a feature piece in a contemporary bathroom, for towels.

Look for hidden potential in old items. Repainting or stripping can transform an old chest, while changing the handles on a wardrobe will give it an instant new look. Pieces like these have great potential in an eclectic environment. They can be combined with other elements in a space, or a single piece can be the focal point in an interior, creating a bold juxtaposition with the architecture or other furniture.

As well as providing infinite options for all kinds of storage, ethnic furniture has a powerful resonance in an ancient and modern interior. A nineteenth-century teak temple cupboard from Rajasthan, for storing china; or a contemporary willow basket from Japan, for vegetables or clothing, adds a primitive simplicity to a modern interior. The key to relocating these items successfully to an ancient and modern environment is to use them for everyday storage.

Office or industrial equipment such as metal filing cabinets, safes, lockers and cabinets can provide useful shelving, hanging and drawer space and brings a contemporary focus to an ancient and modern interior.

Used for storing archives and ephemera, a stack of cardboard boxes on a lightweight metal frame offsets the ancient stonework of this Gothic chapel conversion.

TOP Reinvented as a unit for storing and displaying glasses, this antique cabinet is a practical and appealing feature.
CENTRE A steel bolt set in a wooden batten provides simple but effective storage for an array of kitchen utensils, in keeping with the low-tech aesthetic of a modest wooden house.
BOTTOM Commercial stainless-steel shelving provides heavy-duty open storage for china and glass. The strong lines of each shelf overrule any sense of disorder or clutter.

Modern icons in an ancient space

COMBINING TWENTIETH-CENTURY FURNITURE AND ARCHITECTURAL SALVAGE IN A PARIS APARTMENT

In this two-level apartment in a typical block in central Paris architectural designer Frederic Mechiche has used nineteenth-century architectural salvage to transform a blank space into an interior that provides a dynamic contrast to a collection of iconic twentieth-century furniture and works by contemporary British artists.

The architectural salvage consists of three key structural features: a sweeping staircase with plain wrought-iron banisters, wide worn floorboards throughout the

THIS PAGE Nineteenth-century salvage panelling and bare salvage floorboards provide a setting for twentieth-century furniture such as Barcelona chairs. The informal arrangement of chairs, books and photographs creates a welcoming space for relaxation in a central reception area. OPPOSITE A sweeping staircase, which was also salvaged, is another key architectural feature. Its elegant yet simple form contrasts with iconic twentieth-century furniture.

Mechiche has overlaid the original interior with an alternative style of architecture to evoke a different time and place.

ABOVE A collection of Charles and Ray Eames chairs and two of four identical tables. The tables can be grouped together or separated for different uses and according to the number of people sitting down together.
LEFT Views through openings on either side of the room connect the dining room and main sitting area, yet the two rooms are very different in function and style.
OPPOSITE The texture of the wood panelling provides a historic backdrop to the simple form of a Charles Eames chair. The patinas on the chair, panelling and floorboards mellow the contrasts between the different elements.

apartment and period panelling that lines the walls and was used to reconfigure the space into a series of interconnecting areas and rooms. In effect, Mechiche has overlaid the original interior with an alternative style of architecture to evoke a different time and place. This ambitious transfer works because the architectural salvage is inherently simple and unpretentious.

The entrance to the apartment leads into a central reception area that is also used as a library and for relaxing. Although this area is open and connects with the rest of the space, the impressive staircase and marble fireplace give it status. A sofa, easy chairs and an occasional table create an informal area for sitting and reading. Disorderly piles of books, stacks of photographs and objects on display add to the stimulating and welcoming ambience.

While the staircase is a sculptural feature in its own right, it also provides a practical connection with an upper salon and essential storage space underneath for a collection of books. This architectural solution imposes a degree of order on the collection without preventing easy access to the books themselves.

The room next to the central area is accessible through openings on either side of the fireplace. It is a plain white box with a few well-chosen elements including four identical tables, a collection of classic twentieth-century Eames chairs and a single photograph on the wall. The room borders on the minimal, yet the effect is no less welcoming than that of the previous room. What makes this room distinctive is its flexibility. The tables stand alone or together in different configurations according to requirements. On the day the apartment was photographed for this book a single table was placed beside a window to take advantage of the morning

RIGHT The bedroom and interconnecting bathroom are conventional rooms positioned away from the main living areas and central core of the apartment. The flooring in both is architectural salvage and a change from a wood-block to a tiled floor underlines the separation between the two rooms. The bedroom contains just a bed and a painting, with soft cotton curtains across a wall of windows to diffuse light and provide privacy.

OPPOSITE Central to the arrangement of elements in the bathroom is an antique zinc bath with painted fake wooden sides. The swan-head brass taps complete the elegance of the antique fixtures. Placing a Bertoia chair on either side of the bath continues the juxtaposition of ancient architecture and fixtures and fittings with classic twentieth-century furniture.

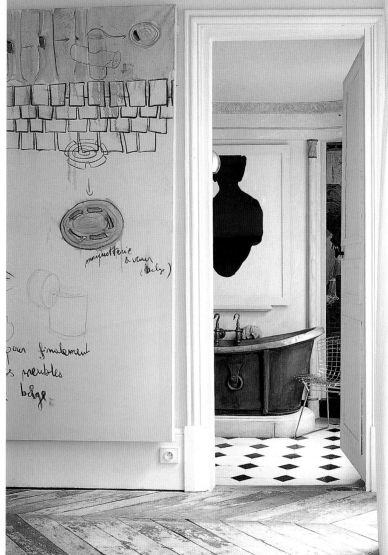

sunlight. Another was on the opposite side of the room with a simple display of two glass vases. The remaining two tables were pushed together in a line between the openings to the central area. For big gatherings the tables form a square in the middle of the room. Chairs are lightweight and easily movable. In keeping with a minimalist aesthetic, double doors lead to a compact high-specification kitchen and a wall panel conceals a cupboard for storing glassware.

The salon upstairs is similar in style and content to the central area, with a collection of twentieth-century furniture including Florence Knoll sofas and Le Corbusier Barcelona chairs. The main difference between the two rooms is that the upper one has a predominantly brown and black colour scheme for textiles and upholstery, and a collection of African tribal art and artefacts is juxtaposed with contemporary photographs.

Away from the general living areas, the bedroom and adjoining bathroom offer sanctuary and seclusion. An antique zinc bath set on a stone base forms an elegant and symmetrical centrepiece to the bathroom, and is surrounded by panelling and a bold black-and-white image. Less pared down than the rest of the apartment, the overall effect in these areas is romantic ancient and modern. The change of pace here contributes as much to the experience of living in the apartment as the change between the main living areas.

Informality and minimalism, books, photographs and objects are all essential aspects of this interior. Yet the success of the overall scheme is to create contrasting and separate areas and not to amalgamate or dilute everything into one overall style. The skill in balancing all the elements and details is evident as you move around the apartment.

Bold eclecticism

POWERFUL COMBINATIONS OF OLD AND NEW IN AN UPDATED EDWARDIAN HOUSE

RIGHT AND OPPOSITE
A pared-down yet warm environment of bare pink plaster walls and limed oak floors throughout the space provides a unifying and flattering backdrop to an eclectic and artful mix of elements and objects. In the sitting area downstairs these include a decorative antique mirror, an ornate chandelier, a contemporary glitter painting, a traditional sofa upholstered in suede and an ethnic wooden table.

The scale and sense of space and light in this semidetached Edwardian house in suburban London bear no relation to its original configuration. It was formerly a typical family house with individual rooms for sitting, eating and cooking, and with four bedrooms and an attic. After its radical conversion by architect J.F. Delsalle the space is now open-plan on two levels with a bathing area on the landing between them. References to everyday Edwardian living – interior walls and architraving, for example – have gone. The ceiling on the ground floor has been raised by 50 centimetres and an industrial staircase designed for a factory connects the two main levels. Yet, with the structure laid bare, the generous proportions of the space become apparent.

The furniture throughout is a mix of individual pieces in traditional, iconic and eccentric designs.

The ground floor is effectively one room that
extends from the front to the back of the house with
dogleg stairs leading to the upper level. Walls and
ceilings are bare pink plaster and the floor is lime-
bleached oak. The big windows, which include a bay
window at the front of the house, and external doors
are the only original Edwardian features. On one
side of the room two nineteenth-century Gothic
stone fireplaces with antique mirrors hung above
them set the standard for an original, eclectic ancient
and modern style.

Powerful combinations of elements – a sculptural
modern chaise longue by Charles and Ray Eames
with an antique wooden bed from Rajasthan, an
antique Italian chandelier that once hung in a church
with a modern artwork, a nineteenth-century
jeweller's worktable with contemporary stainless-
steel restaurant cupboards – add a vital layer of
individuality, shape and colour. Similar confident
juxtapositions and connections of ancient and
modern architectural details, furniture and objects
enliven the whole space.

The furniture throughout is a mix of individual
pieces in traditional, eccentric and iconic designs. In
the sitting area a traditional comfortable English sofa
covered in brown suede, a Jacobean-style armchair
with yellow silk upholstery, a Toshiyuki Kita 'wink'
chair and a decorative Victorian settee form an
appealing collection.

At the back of the ground floor, a step leads down
to a generous cooking and eating area. Along one
wall the entire kitchen slots into an immaculate low-
level white block with a refrigerator and dishwasher
in cupboards, a kitchen sink with laboratory taps, a
work surface and an electric hob. Below the work
surface, open stainless-steel racks – ideal for
saucepans, stacks of white plates and African
wooden bowls – provide most of the storage space.
Foodstuffs are concealed in stainless-steel restaurant
cupboards on the opposite wall. The simplicity of
using either white or stainless steel projects a sense
of order and minimizes the kitchen's visual impact on
the overall space. It also offsets the texture and
shape of the nineteenth-century jeweller's worktable
and the sewing chairs in the dining area. Shaped like
a giant piece from a jigsaw puzzle, and set against a
plain background, the sculptural outline of the table
becomes a key feature.

The upper level is for working, sleeping and
relaxing. Part of the ceiling has been removed and
glass has been fixed into the gable end to create a
distinctive architectural feature and increase the
amount of light in the space. An antique Indian bed
in one corner can be screened with pleated white
plastic dividers designed for commercial use. On the
landing an identical screen provides optional
separation for the combined bathroom, dressing
room and laundry area. The remaining roof space is
an additional compact sleeping area, with ladder
rungs for access and a new skylight.

As well as space and openness, light and reflection
are keynotes in this building. Light from the new
skylights and the glass in the gable end add a
luminosity that filters through the stairs to the
ground floor. Mirrors and glass are positioned to
reflect light. Luxurious white velvet curtains on either
side of the window, a glitter painting on the wall and
silk, velvet and suede upholstery all contribute
shimmering or shining surfaces and finishes.

DETAILS

'God is in the details.'

Mies van der Rohe

THIS PAGE An inspirational
collection of flea-market
finds, personal treasures
and a few well-chosen
objects is displayed on a
row of identical side tables
in Gert van de Keuken's
Paris apartment.
PREVIOUS PAGES The split
and worm-eaten surface of a
worker's bench, found in the
street and now used as a
table, presents a contrasting
and textural backdrop to
contemporary tableware.

Details add an essential layer of colour, texture and shape to a home. Decorative and functional objects, pictures, mirrors, textiles, lights, and fixtures and fittings all play a crucial part in defining an individual ancient and modern style.

Details can be used both in isolation and in combination with other features in a space. Making a single detail the focal point of an interior – for example, a contemporary chandelier made from concrete reinforcing bars and glass beads in a nineteenth-century town house, or an African goat's-milk bowl on a hand-hewn wooden pillar in an Art Deco apartment – creates an effective ancient and modern contrast between a detail and the architectural style of a space. Vibrant antique silk floor cushions on a concrete floor add visual punctuation to a contemporary interior, and positioning a twentieth-century ceramic bowl on the mantel shelf of a Georgian fire surround will bring the special qualities of both into focus.

Juxtapositions between details – used as single features or in compatible groups – and the furniture within a space can be similarly effective and direct. Examples include ancient and modern ethnic textiles, bowls and artefacts with traditional and antique English furniture in a modern loft-style apartment, and antique French decorative mirrors, glass, and silk cushions with contemporary sofas, chairs and tables in a pared-down interior.

Establishing connections between details and the structure of a space or the elements within it creates a very different ancient and modern environment. The collection of details can often include greater diversity but the overall effect is less contrasting. In fashion designer Han Feng's New York loft most of the details and furniture in a former light-industrial space are oriental, which gives the interior a sense of harmony and connection. Yet within various groups of furniture and details there are bright yellow and red silk lanterns, purple and orange silk cushions, decorative wrought-iron birdcages, rustic bamboo stools and tables, twig baskets and delicate lacquered cupboards and boxes.

This chapter shows how details of every kind, from paintings to teapots, can be used to create ancient and modern combinations that will personalize and enrich a home.

Display

Objects, artefacts and pictures offer great potential for creating ancient and modern combinations, and the way they are displayed is an important consideration. Whether it is a collection of glass, ceramics, sculptures, paintings or photographs; an artful cross section of everything; or a single object, a display works well if it has shape, colour and a theme or an idea. It is therefore essential to maintain a sense of discipline both about the items you choose and the way you display them.

If you are combining several different objects, finding out which pieces work well together is a matter of trial and error. When assembling a line of ceramics for display, ceramicist Rupert Spira puts several pots together spontaneously then reviews and edits them in order to achieve the best effect. Style forecaster Gert van de Keuken rarely moves an object once he has put it in his apartment, preferring to trust to his instincts about what is right. Yet some people move objects around endlessly – sometimes displaying them on their own, sometimes grouping them with other artefacts – and discover and enjoy new compositions, juxtapositions and connections every time.

THIS PAGE This powerful juxtaposition of 1970s columns of colourful laminated Plexiglas by Vasa and a restored 1860s marble fire surround is compounded by the minimal environment.
OPPOSITE A bathroom sash-window presents an unusual opportunity for a display. The sandblasted glass diffuses incoming light and masks the view, so attention is focused on the shapes and colours of the decorative glass bottles.

When selecting the object or objects to be displayed it is important to consider the background and base as well as the scale, balance and perspective of the display. For example, a large brown pot on a bamboo stool looks very different to the same pot on an oak chest of drawers. The way lighting affects the colour, shape and texture of different objects is another important factor.

Essentially, displaying an object or a collection of objects provides a means to contain it, which either isolates or connects it with the surroundings. Standing a contemporary plain dinner plate behind an antique Chinese lacquer box, or propping up a square of sandblasted glass behind an ancient object such as a tribal mask, can create an enlivening contrast of colour and texture. Resting a piece of driftwood on a contemporary metal box or pinning a snapshot onto handmade paper provides textural contrasts and gives prominence to ordinary objects. The different styles of frames that contain pictures can either link the images to, or contrast them with, their surroundings. In a contemporary interior with white walls, displaying black-and-white archive prints in white mounts and frames connects them with the structure of the space, whereas in a Georgian home with grey panelled walls colourful modern prints in wooden frames create a contrast. Both contemporary frames and simple old ones work well with modern images, although it can be difficult to find an antique frame that will fit a specific artwork.

Sculptures and other art objects can be contained by their background and setting, which could be a shelf above a fireplace, a deep window recess or a cabinet. The surface on which a display stands is also important. A white shelf on a white wall is a dynamic architectural setting for eighteenth-century black-and-white prints. A former catering trolley with stainless-steel shelves provides a contrasting surface for a group of ancient ceramic bowls.

Objects
The vast range of objects that can be used in displays – anything from decorative items such as sculptures or bowls to utility items like cooking utensils or natural objects such as pebbles or fossils – provides great scope for ancient and modern combinations. Look for links between objects from different periods and develop narratives by placing them together. A collection of wooden artefacts on a stainless-steel console table could include an ancient Japanese bowl, a mid-twentieth-century pot and an Arts and Crafts box containing fragments of bones. A collection of ancient and modern glass candlesticks could be placed on a mantel-shelf. A display of identical objects – such as a string of contemporary papier-mâché lanterns ranged down the centre of an ancient farmhouse table – can have great impact.

RIGHT Displaying shells, wishbones and small fragile items in a decorative antique glass protects them from damage and dispels a sense of clutter.
OPPOSITE Using a large glass vase to contain and display treasures like this animal skull and archive print is an effective way of combining disparate objects. The photographic print is by Simon Upton.

Natural objects like a sculptural branch, pebbles or a collection of fossils can be as decorative as handmade ones. Interweave them with other objects in a display, or group small ones together. Create unusual combinations, such as shells in an antique ebony bowl or a piece of flint in a glass fish bowl.

The fact that old utensils like wooden spoons, chopping boards, wire sieves and copper pots are designed to be used with ease, and are made from natural materials, explains why they are still used in contemporary kitchens. Along with china, cutlery and glass from antique and junk shops they already provide an ancient element in many modern households. To highlight the juxtaposition, store ancient pots and frying pans, sieves and casserole dishes on streamlined stainless-steel shelving and keep old wooden spoons in a stainless-steel measuring jug.

If you want to display china and glassware in your kitchen, consider any ancient and modern combinations in the overall context of the space. For example, if you have an antique dresser or painted cupboard, this is an ideal place to display contemporary china and glassware, or a mix of antique and contemporary tableware. A collection of old and new china, cutlery and glass will enable you to create ancient and modern table settings.

Old utility items work well in other areas of an ancient and modern space. Wooden boxes in a work area for storing desktop equipment, baskets in a bedroom for organizing clothes, and storage jars in a bathroom for herbal remedies are examples.

The text visible in the image reads:

LA PORTE MAG...

TI·CLAVDIVS·DRVSIF·CAESAR·AVG...
TRIBVNICIA·POTESTATE·XII·COS·VIN...
EX·ONDAM·EX·FONTIBVS·QVI·VOCABANTVR·NO...
ITEM·ANIENEM·NOVAM·A·MILLIARIO·LXII·VENERVNT...

C·CAESAR·DIVI·VESPASIANVS·AVGVST·PONTIF·MAXIM...
TEM·VETIAM·ET·CAERVLEAM·FERDVCTI·IVBEN·VC...
PER·ANNOS·NOVEM·IVBEN·F...

C·CAESAR·DIVI·F·VESPASIANVS·AVGVST·PON...
POTESTATE·L·IMPERATOR·AVGVST·X·VIII...
DVANDAM·CVRAVIT·ETIAM·ET...
···AERVLEAM·FH...

This eclectic display of sparkly and reflective blue objects is an oasis of contrast and detail in a pared-down space with bare pink plaster walls and limed-oak floors. The romance and decoration of the arrangement is balanced by the neutral surface of an ancient Indian table.

The temporariness of this spontaneous collection is part of its appeal. With a cupboard full of individual mismatching items, every meal and tea-break has the potential to look different from the previous one. The shape of the chopping board used as a teatray underlines the curves and roundness of the china cups and teapot.

The bold shape of this stainless-steel commercial cupboard provides high-specification kitchen storage and overrides any sense of clutter about the collection of Indian aluminium food pots on top. Distracting and discordant food packages are hidden behind sliding doors, ensuring the kitchen area remains monochromatic.

d ephemeral as the combinations of cutlery and china you choose when you lay a table
an arrangement of antique glass or ceramics.

The shape and texture of this Moroccan tea table provides an ancient ethnic juxtaposition to a spacious New York loft. The antique Moroccan teapot and traditional glasses are functional as well as decorative.

Every item of antique or second-hand glass on these shelves is animated by light from an adjacent window. In contrast to the delicate and reflective glass, a collection of found objects such as a bird's nest and pebbles seems well-defined and prominent. The strong lines of the architectural shelving contain the display.

Textiles

Textiles such as rugs, cushions, throws, blankets, curtains and blinds soften the hard lines and bare surfaces of structural features and furniture and help to make an ancient and modern environment warm and welcoming. Even simple ideas can have great impact: laying a contemporary grey felt rug on ancient floorboards to provide a soft base in a relaxing area, for example, or hanging a modern muslin drape in front of an imposing stone-arch window to diffuse light and screen a view. An antique silk cushion on a contemporary modular sofa, or a modern ethnic cushion on a worn velvet chesterfield, adds visual and textural contrast as well as extra softness to firm pieces of furniture.

ABOVE Placing an antique Indian silk bolster on a contemporary tweedy sofa brings out the colour and weave of the fabrics and adds an additional layer of comfort.
RIGHT Used in Morocco for making hats, these metre squares of red and blue-black felt have been sewn together with other squares to create a striking bedcover.

This African kuba cloth consists of complex graphic shapes sewn together. Shown off to good effect as a banner hanging from a mezzanine level in a studio, it provides separation between different areas.

ABOVE Curtains in this industrial conversion are a seasonal 'hibernation' detail. Lengths of muslin hung over steel tubing are easily removed in spring.

RIGHT This is the flip side of a cowhide, painted with white paint. This way up it is a simple graphic shape that adds a change of texture on a concrete floor and defines a seating area.

BELOW In this New York loft with concrete flooring and plain white walls the seating area consists of big cushions covered in traditional Moroccan fabrics. The combination of pattern, colour and shape works well in this environment.

Natural textiles like wool, silk, cotton and linen are good options for window treatments, cushions and throws as they fade and soften with use.

Ornate wrought-iron curtain poles are an unusual decorative detail in this pared-down nineteenth-century church conversion, yet are in perfect balance with the scale of the space.

Ancient textiles include old kilims, Persian rugs, cowhides, linen sheets, wool blankets, brocades, velvet cushions, ethnic fabrics and hand-sewn and hand-printed silks, cottons and linen. Select old textiles carefully to suit the use and location. A hard-wearing kilim runner or a Persian wool rug will stand up to everyday wear and tear in a living area. An antique quilt, on the other hand, is best used as a decorative daytime cover for a bed rather than as a practical alternative to a duvet or blanket.

Ancient and modern textiles can be combined in the same item. Examples include attaching a canvas heading to an antique linen sheet to make a curtain, combining antique silk with cotton to make bolsters, or using old linen on one side of a cushion and a contemporary hand-knitted square or piece of suede on the other side. If necessary, worn antique fabrics can be repaired by using contemporary unbleached canvas, leather, cotton lining or ticking as a backing.

Natural textiles like wool, silk, cotton and linen are good options for window treatments, cushions and throws as they fade and soften with use. This adds a valuable layer of colour and texture to a space and their visual effect is similar to that of genuinely ancient fabrics. For the same reason, carpets and rugs in these materials make excellent floor coverings. Rush or coir matting is another good choice. In a factory conversion with bare brick walls and concrete floors this natural material is compatible with the ambience and texture of the structural ones. Contemporary matting can also be used as a contrast to ancient elements in a space – on polished floorboards in a living area, for example.

Ancient ethnic textiles enliven contemporary interiors with colour, contrast, pattern and cultural references. Examples include a silk quilt or vibrant Moroccan fabric used as a throw on a minimalist modern sofa, or an Indian sari hung between the living and eating areas in an open-plan space. Antique kilims work well on bare boards in both modern and ancient environments and also make good cushion covers and throws. The fading colours of hand-dyed textiles like kilims and quilts combine brilliantly with the natural colours and textures of plain bare walls and floors, whether these are brick, stone, wood or plaster.

Mirrors

Mirrors are practical and decorative, and can add an extra architectural detail or change the view within an ancient and modern environment.

Practically, mirrors are vital features in bathing and dressing areas, and anywhere else where it is useful to see your reflection. They also help to optimize the sense of light in a space.

Decoratively, they can be used to enliven a plain wall. For example, an antique French mirror could be leaned against a bare plaster wall. Or they can provide a focal point – a contemporary mirror cut to the same width as a Victorian fireplace, mounted in a plain frame and hung above the mantel shelf will draw attention to the combination of old and new elements. Antique mirrors, in plain or ornate frames, always look good and can be used in both ancient and modern environments in many different ways.

Architecturally, mirrors can extend an interior with views beyond the existing structure. Placing a mirror to reflect daylight from a window or skylight will instantly alter the perspective and quality of light in a space. Experiment with different positions to find the right

one. You can also position a mirror to reflect a key architectural feature. For example, a contemporary mirror could be placed to reflect a curving eighteenth-century staircase or exposed brickwork.

Using a simple sheet of mirror glass without a frame blurs the separation between it and the surface it is hanging on or leaning against. The mirror becomes a simple geometric shape that adds a dynamic detail and fits in with any style of architecture, ancient or modern. Examples are a rectangle of mirror glass in an eighteenth-century building, installed above an original mantelpiece and reflecting a window; or a circle of glass in a twentieth-century home, hung on a blue wall yet reflecting a yellow one. Mirrors like these present a perfect pool of reflection in contrast to the surface around them and can be cut to any shape or size. Antique mirrors that have been removed from their frames can be used in the same way.

On a smaller scale a mirror placed behind a favourite ceramic or wooden carving will enhance the presentation of the object with alternative views and reflected light. Mirror panels fixed to the wall behind a display shelf will have a similar effect.

THIS PAGE An antique bathroom mirror with a plain frame sets the style of understatement and fine detailing in a New York loft. The basin and mirror configuration is one of a pair, set side by side along a wall of gray and white marble.
OPPOSITE This ornate mirror is positioned above a fireplace in an open-plan living area to reflect ambient light. Framing the reflection of an industrial staircase is a bonus.

Pictures

A painting, a photograph or a two-dimensional piece of artwork like a collage can provide a single key focal point in an ancient and modern space, or it can be used to define an area within an interior. An example of the latter is a series of Perspex box-framed archive postcards placed alongside an antique dining table in a modern extension to an Edwardian house.

Planning how and where to display a picture, whether it is a limited edition contemporary print, a family photograph or a nineteenth-century oil painting, is about balancing it with its surroundings – ideally to the benefit of both. The three main points to consider are the content, colour and size of the work; the surface it will be displayed against; and the frame – all of which provide scope for ancient and modern juxtapositions or connections. For example, hanging an ancient, predominantly brown oil painting on a grey-painted wall in a contemporary space will add clarity and definition to the work.

The frame can be used either to connect a picture with its surroundings or to separate it from them. For example, a contemporary painting in muted colours could be framed in light wood to complement the image and make a visual connection with ancient wooden furniture. A modern black-and-white photograph combined with a plain white mount will add a dynamic contrast to an all-white contemporary interior.

Using identical frames and mounts will unify different kinds of artwork, such as a collection of ancient and modern pencil sketches, oil paintings and watercolours, without detracting from their content. Framing similar images in mismatching antique frames – for example a series of contemporary black-and-white family photographs in odd wooden frames – creates a lively display.

ABOVE The horizontal lines of a long ad hoc table and exposed ceiling contain – and therefore frame – these abstract horizontal landscape paintings in ceramicist Rupert Spira's Shropshire farmhouse.
RIGHT Displayed without an ornate gilt frame, a traditional oil painting looks refreshingly strong, direct and modern.

ABOVE The presentation, position and scale of this photograph of a chair made by artists Langlands and Bell makes a dynamic exhibition feature in their London house.
BELOW When hanging a picture it is important to take into account the other elements in the room. The size and position of this antique table and contemporary painting balance each other.

Lighting

The right kind of lighting can transform the atmosphere in your home, and introduce variation and contrast throughout a space. For example, it could be diffused in a dining or relaxing area and bright and direct in a work space. Planning and installing a comprehensive lighting system will reflect your individual style, contribute to the atmosphere of a space and allow you to position or implement appropriate fittings. For instance, including power sockets in the floor will give you the flexibility to move lights around, and is especially useful in large open-plan spaces.

Essentially, lighting falls into four categories. Ambient lighting is general background lighting that throws light over a wide area. Task lighting illuminates a specific activity. Accent lighting is used to highlight an architectural feature or painting. Information lighting maps out a space or illuminates a passageway or a change in floor level. It is therefore important to think about the kind of effects you want as well as the style of light fittings. (It is always a good idea to review lighting whenever you carry out

MAIN PICTURE Scale is an important factor in finding an appropriate central light fitting. In this New York loft, where everything is out-size, a spaceship lantern looms over an interconnecting studio and living space.
LEFT The classic shape and design of a bare light bulb, hooked onto a beam and hanging low over a kitchen table, is in keeping with a raw industrial space.

any structural alterations or decoration, as this presents an opportunity to extend or replace an existing system without additional disruption and expense.)

Ancient fittings, which are often decorative or grandiose, are ideal as ambient lighting and can become a focal point in a space. Central fittings like antique chandeliers and glass pendants offer lots of potential for adding an enlivening detail to an ancient and modern interior. In Yvonne Sporre's unconventional Edwardian town house, for example, a teardrop church chandelier with the letter 'M' (for Madonna) engraved on each crystal leaf makes a romantic central feature. In artists Langlands and Bell's modest London home, traditional glass pendants provide a simpler central fitting in keeping with a minimal historic environment.

Antique table and standard lamps add shape, colour and variation to a space as well as satellite pools of light – either in conjunction with other, possibly contemporary, fittings or as an independent option. In a New York loft a baroque table lamp with a yellow silk shade and pear-shaped crimson glass base makes a magical focal point on a junk-shop side table. In an alternative setting, also in New York, standard lamps with quirky Victorian black stands and simple parchment shades present mellow ambient options in a dining area and bedroom.

In general ancient lighting is low-tech and decorative. It provides few opportunities for accent, task and information lighting, and therefore works well in conjunction with a modern system. However, one option for old task lighting is ex-commercial lights – former office, surgical or film lights, for example. A row of ex-office anglepoise lamps mounted above a kitchen work-surface in a Victorian mansion-block apartment in London is a practical re-use of a design classic. In Jonathan Leitersdorf's New York loft, a row of chrome anglepoise lamps stored on top of a cabinet, awaiting use elsewhere, makes an unusually decorative display.

For performance, efficiency and design, modern fittings work well in all four categories of lighting and are a practical, adaptable and often exhilarating option for all kinds of architectural styles. Unobtrusive recess lights, track lights and bare-wire lighting (parallel bare wires with miniature spotlights fixed to, or hanging off, the wires) are good options for ambient lighting. Big impact contemporary designs make exciting features in ancient and modern interiors. Examples include a mass of bare bulbs jangling from a fan of fine wires in a Georgian sitting room, and oversized woven paper drums in a converted factory with bare brick walls. Sculptural plastic shapes, glass tubes and paper globes, which glow or radiate an even light, enliven a space and provide useful satellite lighting, on either the floor or low tables. They also create dynamic juxtapositions with ancient structures, surfaces and elements. Many contemporary standard lamps are wonderful architectural objects in their own right and are ideal for task lighting – for example, as reading lights.

If you prefer low-level light, possibly because this is in keeping with the original intention or historic style of a space, or simply for variation, install dimmer switches or controls as standard with all fittings.

There are many different ways to adapt antique fittings. An oil-lamp or candle-holding chandelier can be rewired to work on electricity, for example, and there are many different ways to update or extend existing systems. If you have any concerns about the safety of a light or a system, or if you need advice about updating a system, ask an electrician. To find out about new designs and systems, visit a lighting showroom; some offer a free design service.

RIGHT A clip-on spotlight above a mirror is a low-tech solution for essential task lighting in a bathroom.
FAR RIGHT A contemporary 'Jack' light by Tom Dixon adds a graphic form as well as variation in lighting to a New York loft.
BELOW In keeping with a new direction in lighting design characterized by simple shapes in white glass or opaque plastic, this globe is a key accent light in a simple bedroom.
BELOW RIGHT Japanese paper lanterns come in all shapes and sizes, from collectable Noguchi originals to inexpensive alternatives from high-street stores. This one is in a former spice factory in New York.

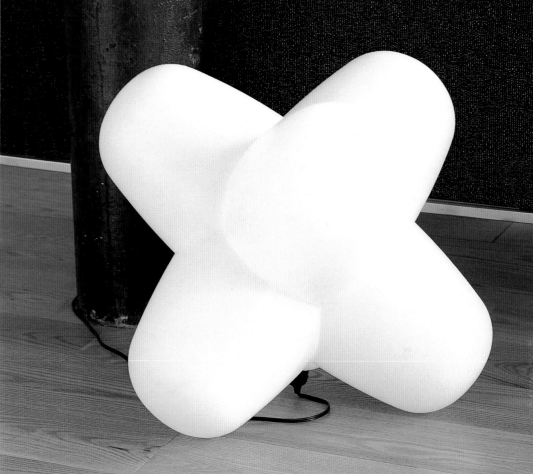

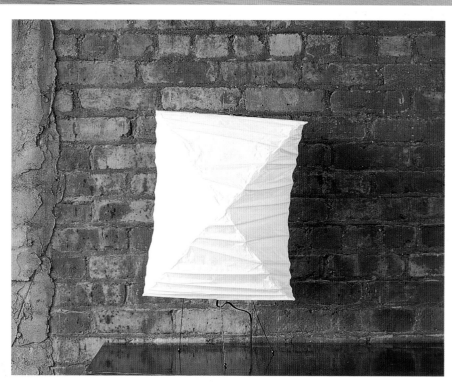

Fixtures and fittings

By definition fixtures and fittings, such as kitchen sinks, baths, kitchen and bathroom taps, light switches, door handles, radiators and built-in shelving, are permanent integral details within a space, essential to how your home looks, feels and functions. This applies whether you want to leave in place or restore original fixtures and fittings, such as a cast-iron roll-top bath; use architectural salvage fixtures and fittings from the same or a different period of architecture, such as cast-iron radiators; or find contemporary alternatives, like stainless-steel laboratory mixer taps.

Original storage fixtures are always a bonus, especially an understair cupboard or kitchen pantry that does not extend into valuable living space. Wooden built-in shelving or cupboards provide low-key structural storage solutions that are as visually appealing as they are efficient, and may have had so many coats of paint that they have become conjoined to the surrounding architectural structure. If you are fitting new shelving it is worth using seasoned wood to avoid cracks and splits. If you plan to leave the wood bare, weathered or bleached boards fit in well with any style of architecture. Choose low-key support brackets or frames to keep the focus on the patina and texture of the wood and on any connection or juxtaposition with the structure of the space.

Changing handles on doors and cupboards, for example by introducing tubular aluminium D handles, is a simple way to update a space. As you are likely to be replacing ancient with modern, and not vice versa, remove just one handle as a tester and check alternatives before you commit to changing all of them. The worn smoothness of a wooden handle on a kitchen cupboard may take some giving up!

If you inherit antique plumbing fixtures and fittings like cast-iron radiators, you can use them to create a classic juxtaposition with a contemporary structural element or piece of furniture – a concrete floor, for example, or a glass and metal dining table. Antique or salvaged plumbing adds a sense of history to an interior and often has an appealing chunky design. Mixing ancient and modern plumbing fixtures is relatively easy as pipe sizes are generally standardized. Even if there is a mismatch with pipe or drain sizes, it is usually possible to work around any incompatibility so you can fit any style of radiator, sink, bath or taps. It is always important to check for signs of erosion. If you buy salvaged plumbing fixtures and fittings, do so on the condition that you can swap them if they don't work.

The appeal of salvaged or antique taps is their worn, smooth surfaces. However, make sure you choose taps that are in proportion to the size of your sink, basin or bath – some oversized antique designs overpower modern bath- or kitchenware. In general, decorative taps look great in bathing areas; utility taps work well in kitchen areas. Juxtapositions between different fixtures and fittings, for example a traditional butler's kitchen sink with a mono-block tap, avoids predictable period styling and delivers high-tech efficiency to a hard-working area.

LEFT Everything for this low-tech kitchen sink unit was found or bought locally. Wood for the draining board was found in the barn, and the local hardware store did not have matching plugs in stock. **RIGHT** The industrial look of a stainless-steel commercial cooker makes it an ideal stand-alone piece of kitchen equipment. To avoid a cluttered kitchen choose a design with a built-in splashback and shelf to store cooking oils.

Antique or salvaged plumbing adds a sense of history to an interior and often has an appealing chunky design.

Although a traditional radiator always looks good, painting it the same colour as the wall is the best option and designates it as a low-key architectural fixture. This one makes an alternative light stand.

LEFT Natural materials like blue-grey riven slate tiles and wood and paper shoji screens offset shining chrome bathroom fixtures and fittings.
FAR LEFT This swan-head mixer tap is antique, yet the hot and cold levers are part of a new system. It is usually possible to find a way to combine the aesthetics of antique fittings with the efficiency and performance of modern ones.

Collection and display

PERSONALIZING A SPLIT-LEVEL APARTMENT WITH A MIX OF FURNITURE AND DETAILS

LEFT Textiles in natural dyes, contemporary tube lighting and ethnic objects in raw wood contribute shape, colour and meaning to the space.

BELOW LEFT Once used as a container for goat's milk, this African bowl is a compelling central detail in the apartment.

OPPOSITE A simple painted pine table, found in a dustbin and previously used for dining, is now used for display. A friend's sculpture and a china hare reflect the owner's passion for combining the simple with the baroque.

This split-level Art Deco apartment is on the top floor of a 1920s block in Paris, originally designed to provide living and working spaces for artists. Although the apartment is compact, the interior is well planned, organized to perfection and full of light. White walls, painted concrete floors and minimal architectural detailing provide a strong, clean backdrop for individual elements and objects that have meaning for, and give enjoyment to, the style forecaster Gert van de Keuken who lives here.

The economical configuration of the space includes a double-height studio. This has a wall of windows and these, and the view, are the first things you see when you enter the apartment. They are an important architectural feature with access to a terrace and provide a source of light powerful enough to even out any day-to-day scuffs so that the interior looks positively pristine.

The studio occupies approximately two-thirds of the space and is the main living area. It also provides essential access to the upper level. Various groups of furniture focus on different activities. For example, modern black iron chairs by Harry Bertoia standing on the white-painted reverse side of a cowhide provide a more formal seating area than a bench almost hidden under the stairs with sheepskins on a base of felt pads and colourful cushions made from Moroccan fabrics. Between the windows and the stairs there is a traditional desk with papers and correspondence, and a flea-market table and two facing chairs stand by the door towards the back of the studio. The shape and orientation of the space mean there is the freedom to organize and use it in many different ways, and without seeming contrived or leaving an obvious passageway these focus groups of furniture allow easy movement through the studio.

At the back of the space, on the lower level, there are a bedroom, bathroom and dressing room separated from the studio by folding doors with glass panels. Open stairs lead to the eating area on the upper level. In part an open terrace, with a balcony like an internal bay window, this overlooks the studio and has a view through the windows. This is very different to the view from the lower level: there is more sky and less intrusion from nearby buildings. The dining table is a wooden workbench that was found in the street. Equally narrow benches from a flea market, and Thonet chairs, originally designed in the late 1850s, provide seating. Behind a wall, the adjoining kitchen extends the full width of the space.

Unlike some apartments in the block, where the terrace is enclosed to make a bedroom, this one retains its original open-plan structure and a sense of connection between the terrace and the main studio.

Just as it is the nature of this space to be visible and open, any elements or details within it are easy to see and accessible. Part of the enjoyment of the objects on display is their cultural diversity – they include an African bowl for goat's milk, an English painting and a Japanese ceramic. Chosen for their shapes and what they mean to the owner, and placed by instinct, nothing seems overworked or academic. The objects are not necessarily valuable, yet they reveal the love and appreciation of the person who brought them together.

Ancient and modern ethnic details – especially from Morocco and Africa – are important. Taking an object away from the culture that created it and contrasting it with contemporary architecture focuses attention on the piece: a Moroccan tea table, for example, scraps of felt made into a bedcover, an African milking stool or wooden figure. Equally, finding a twig sculpture in a street market in Paris and mixing it with a modern Jean Cocteau ceramic creates a refreshing contrast.

Even accidental and everyday combinations – a table set with Japanese ceramic beakers and Swedish dinner plates, for example – make as vital and pleasurable a contribution to the interior as a display of a beach pebble and a piece of sculpture on a pine table. The open-plan arrangement of the space, and the blank canvas it provides, creates the opportunity to put together compositions or accidental groupings of objects, textiles and lighting on a relatively large scale.

THIS PAGE The simple structure of white walls and a beige-painted concrete floor provides a strong backdrop to an individual collection of furniture, art, artefacts and textiles. Despite a sense of order, the juxtaposition and arrangement of details add a casualness. The owner rarely moves things once he has put them down.

OPPOSITE LEFT Making good use of a semiconcealed space under the stairs, a new built-in bench provides a base for a home-made daybed with soft sheepskins on top of felt pads, and cushions made from Moroccan fabrics. The round tables are also from Morocco.

OPPOSITE RIGHT Mixing the colours and shapes of second-hand and contemporary elements, this table setting illustrates the owner's joy and natural ease in putting different objects together.

RESOURCES

Contributors

The following is a list of those whose work was photographed for this book or who supplied products for photography.

ARCHITECTS AND ARCHITECTURAL DESIGNERS

Frederic Mechiche
4 Rue de Thorigny
75003 Paris
France
Tel: 0033 1 4278 7828

J.F. Delsalle
3 Rue Seguier
75006 Paris
France
Tel: 0033 1 4329 4276

Jonathan Leitersdorf
Just Design Ltd
80 Fifth Avenue
18th Floor
New York, NY 10011
Tel: 001 212 243 6544

Pierre D'Avoine Architects
6A Orde Hall Street
London WC1 N3JW
Tel: 020 7242 2124

Smith-Miller + Hawkinson
Architects LLP
305 Canal Street, 4th Floor
New York, NY 10013
USA
Tel: 001 212 966 3875

Stephen Roberts Inc.
270 Lafayette Street
New York, NY 10012
USA
Tel: 001 212 966 6930

Stickland Combe Architecture
258 Lavender Hill
London SW11 1LJ
Tel: 020 7924 1699

Ushida Findlay (UK) Ltd
94 Leonard Street
London EC2A 4RH
Tel: 020 7613 4972

ARTISTS AND MAKERS

Elena Colombo, sculptor,
New York
Tel: 001 212 334 5069

Ben Langlands and Nikki Bell,
artists, UK
Tel/Fax: 020 7375 2132

Rupert Spira, ceramicist, UK
Tel: 01588 650 588

PRODUCT SUPPLIERS

Michael Benevento
515 Broadway
New York, NY 10012
Tel: 001 212 965 8617
1940s and 1950s furniture by Jean Prouvé, Charlotte Perriand, Le Corbusier and Pierre Jeanneret.

The Dining Room Shop
62–64 White Hart Lane
London SW13 0PZ
Tel: 020 8878 1020
Extensive selection of antique tables, chairs and tableware.

Totem Design Group LLC
71 Franklin Street
New York, NY 10013
Tel: 001 212 925 5506
Contemporary furniture, lighting, textiles and accessories.

OTHER ARCHITECTS

Examples of work by the following architects and designers are included in the text.

Azman Owens Architects
8 St Albans Place
London N1 ONX
Tel: 020 7354 2955

Claire Bataille & Paul Ibens
Vekestraat 13 Bus 14
2000 Antwerp
Belgium
Tel: 0032 3 213 86 20

Fernlund and Logan
414 Broadway
New York, NY10013
USA
Tel: 001 212 925 9628

Fiona Naylor of Johnson Naylor
13 Britton Street
London EC1M 5SX
Tel: 020 7490 8885

Jonathan Ball
5 Belle View
Bude
Cornwall EX23 8JJ
Tel: 01288 355 557

John Pawson
Unit B
70–78 York Way
London N1 9AG
Tel: 020 7837 2929

Lot/ek
55 Little West 12th St
New York, NY 10014
USA
Tel: 001 212 255 9326

Nik Randall of Brookes Stacey Randall
New Hibernia House
Winchester Walk
London SE1 9AG
Tel: 020 7403 0707

Pip Horne
329 Portobello Road
London W10 5RU
Tel: 020 8960 8364

Advice

Architects Registration Board
73 Hallam Street
London W1N 6EE
Tel: 020 7580 5861
Maintains a register of qualified architects.

The Federation of Master Builders
14–15 Great James Street
London WC1N 3DP
Tel: 020 7242 7583
Maintains a register of building firms that do domestic work.

All members are given a membership card, so check with the Federation or ask to see the card.

Royal Institute of British Architects
66 Portland Place
London W1N 4AD
Tel: 020 7307 3700
RIBA's Clients Advisory Service operates an extensive database of RIBA-registered practices. It can also put you in touch with an architect who practises in your area and give you advice on commissioning and briefing an architect. Note, however, that not all qualitifed architects register with the RIBA.

Retailers and suppliers

The following is a selection of retailers and suppliers of a wide range of products appropriate for an ancient and modern interior. If you are planning to make a big investment, set a realistic budget and visit showrooms, manufacturers, independent designers or dealers to see what is available. Check with suppliers for information about nationwide stockists, mail order and websites. If you are looking for a specific ancient, modern or recycled piece it is a good idea to set yourself a time limit to keep the interior of your home progressing towards some kind of resolution. Meanwhile, try to remain open to alternatives. Auctions are a good source of antique items and modern collectible pieces, although it is advisable to check with a specialist or dealer before making a big investment. It is also worth visiting antiques fairs, flea markets and junk shops for ancient items.

FLOORING

Christopher Farr
212 Westbourne Grove
London W11 2RH
Tel : 0207 916 7690
Contemporary and antique hand-made rugs.

Crucial Trading
79 Westbourne Park Road
London W2 5QH
Tel: 0207 221 9000 or 01562 825656 for catalogue and samples
Natural fibre floorcoverings.

Dalsouple
Tel: 01984 667233
Tel: 01984 667551 for stockists
Rubber flooring tiles in an extensive range of colours.

Delabole Slate
Pengelly Road
Delabole
Cornwall PL33 9AZ
Tel: 01840 212242
Slate slabs for flooring, worksurfaces and fireplaces.

Gooding Aluminium
1 British Wharf
Landmann Way
London SE14 5RS
Tel: 020 8692 2255
Sheet aluminium flooring.

The Hardwood Flooring Company
146–152 West End Lane
London NW6 1SD
Tel: 020 7328 8481
New and reclaimed hardwood floors and worktops.

Lassco
41 Maltby Street
London SE1 3PA
Tel: 020 7237 4488 or 020 7749 9944
Reclaimed timber flooring.

Robert Stephenson
1 Elyston Street
Chelsea Green
London SW3 3NT
Tel: 020 7225 2343
Antique rugs.

Sinclair Till
793 Wandsworth Road
London SW8 3JQ
Tel: 020 7720 0031
All types of flooring, including cut-linoleum designs and rugs.

PAINTS

Arts & Crafts Home
28 Gloucester Road
North Laines
Brighton BN14AQ
Tel: 01273 6000073
Charleston paint range, also Arts and Crafts furniture, lighting, antiques and textiles.

Farrow & Ball
Uddens Estate
Wimborne
Dorset BH21 7NL
Tel: 01202 876141
Manfacturers of traditional papers and paints.

John Oliver
33 Pembridge Road
London W11 3HG
Tel : 020 7221 6466
Good range of historic colours.

FURNITURE, LIGHTING AND ACCESSORIES

Antique, second-hand and period designs

After Noah
121 Upper Street
London N1 1QP
Tel: 020 7359 4281
Former classroom, church and factory furniture and fittings.

Alfie's Antique Market
13–25 Church Street
London NW8 8DT
Tel: 020 7723 6066
Over 250 traders selling furniture, lighting, ceramics, glass, kitchenware, textiles, picture frames and many other items.

Clayton Munroe
Kingston West Drive
Kingston
Staverton
Devon TQ9 6AR
Tel: 01803 762626
Period bronze door furniture in a selection of finishes including chrome and nickel.

David Champion
199 Westbourne Grove
London W11 2SB
Tel: 020 7727 6016
Focal pieces of ancient furniture, such as cupboards and tables, and accessories.

Decorative Living
55 New King's Road
London SW6 4SE
Tel: 020 7736 5623
Eclectic ranges including painted cupboards, chests and tables.

Josephine Ryan Antiques
63 Abbeville Road
London SW14 9JW
Tel: 020 8675 3900
Nineteenth-century French and English furniture.

Joss Graham
10 Eccleston Street
London SW1W 9LT
Tel: 020 7730 4370
Ethnic fabrics and accessories.

Judy Greenwood Antiques
657 Fulham Road
London SW6 5PY
Tel: 020 7736 6037
French antiques, beds and textiles.

Lots Road Auction Galleries
71–73 Lots Road
Chelsea SW10
Tel: 020 7351 7771
Specialist sales of antique and twentieth-century modern classic furniture and objects.

Mark Maynard Antiques
651 Fulham Road
London SW6 5PU
Tel: 020 7731 3533
Various styles, including country pieces and painted furniture.

Tobias and the Angel
68 Whitehart Lane
Barnes SW13 0PZ
Tel: 020 8878 8902
Country-style furniture, antique linen, new bedlinen and ceramics.

Twentieth-century iconic designs

Century Design
68 Marylebone High Street
London W1M 3AQ
Tel: 020 7487 5100
Mid-twentieth-century furniture by British and American designers.

TomTom
42 New Compton Street
London WC2H 8DA
Tel: 020 7240 7909
Sixties and seventies 'pop' furniture.

twentytwentyone
274 Upper Street
London N1 2UA
Tel: 020 7288 1996
Mid-twentieth-century classics.

Vitra
30 Clerkenwell Road
London EC1M 5PG
Tel: 020 7608 6200
Modern classic and contemporary furniture.

Contemporary designs

Aero
96 Westbourne Grove
London W2 5RT
020 7221 1950
Furniture and accessories.

The Conran Shop
Michelin House
81 Fulham Road
London SW3 6RD
Tel: 020 7589 7401
Predominantly contemporary furniture with some ethnic and antique pieces, plus lighting, textiles and accessories.

David Mellor
4 Sloane Square
London SW1 8EE
Tel: 020 7730 4259
Kitchen and tableware including modern classic cutlery.

Habitat
196 Tottenham Court Road
London W1P 9LD
Tel: 020 7255 2545
Tel: 0845 601 0740 for details of other branches.
Seasonal collections of reasonably priced contemporary furniture and accessories.

Heal's
196 Tottenham Court Road
London W1P 9LD
Tel: 020 7636 1666
Contemporary furniture, kitchens, lighting, textiles and housewares.

IKEA
For branch information:
Head Office
IKEA Brent Park
2 Drury Way
North Circular Road
London NW10 0TH
Tel: 020 8208 5600
Reasonably priced contemporary furniture and accessories.

John Lewis
278–306 Oxford Street
London W1E 5NN
Tel: 020 7828 1000 for details of branches
Selection of industrial-style kitchen appliances and good basic housewares.

The Holding Company
243–245 King's Road
London SW3 5EL
Tel: 020 7352 1600
Comprehensive range of storage solutions.

London Lighting Company
135 Fulham Road
London SW3 5EW
Tel: 020 7589 3612
Contemporary lighting, including a good range of floor lamps.

Muji
187 Oxford Street
London W1
Tel: 020 7437 7503
Tel: 020 7323 2208 for details of other branches
Metal, carboard and plastic storage units, tableware and bedding.

Purves and Purves
80–81 Tottenham Court Road
London W1P 9HD
Tel: 020 7580 8223
Contemporary furniture, lighting and accessories.

SCP
135 Curtain Road
London EC2A 3BX
Tel: 020 7739 1869
Furniture, lighting and accessories by contemporary European designers.

Skandium
72 Wigmore Street
London W1H 9DL
Tel: 020 7935 2077
Contemporary Scandinavian furniture, lighting, accessories and textiles.

SKK
34 Lexington Street
London W1F 0LH
Tel: 020 7434 4095
Architectural lighting consultancy and stockists of lighting by new designers.

Space
214 Westbourne Grove
London W11 2RH
Tel: 020 7229 6533
Eclectic collection of contemporary furniture and accessories by new designers.

Viaduct
1–10 Summers Street
London EC1R 5BD
Tel: 020 7278 8456
Furniture, lighting and accessories by contemporary European designers.

INDEX

Ethnic designs

David Wainwright
251 Portobello Road
London W11 1LT
Tel: 020 7792 1988
Indian furniture and accessories.

Albrissi
1 Sloane Square
London SW1W 8EE
Tel: 020 7730 6119
*Ancient ethnic furniture and
contemporary furniture with an
ethnic influence.*

**KITCHEN AND BATHROOM
FIXTURES AND FITTINGS**

Aga Rayburn
P.O. Box 30
Ketley
Telford TF1 4DD
Tel: 01952 642000
Traditional ovens and stoves.

Aston Matthews
141–147a Essex Road
London N1 2SN
Tel: 020 7226 3657
*Traditional and contemporary
bathroom furniture.*

Baumatic
3 Elgar Industrial Estate
Preston Road
Reading RG2 0BE
Tel: 0118 9310055
Industrial-style cookers.

Bulthaup UK Ltd
37 Wigmore Street
London W1H 9LD
Tel: 020 7495 3663
*High-specification 'total'
kitchens.*

Buyers and Sellers
120 Ladbroke Grove
London W10 5NE
Tel: 020 7229 1947
*Leading-brand appliances for
kitchens and bathrooms at
good prices.*

C.P. Hart
Newnham Terrace
Hercules Road
London SE1 7DR
Tel: 020 7902 1000
*Traditional and contemporary
designs for kitchens and
bathrooms.*

Czech & Speake
125 Fulham Road
London SW3 6RT
Tel: 020 7225 3667
*Traditional and classic designs
for kitchens and bathrooms*

Hansgrohe
Units D1 & D2 Sandown Park
Trading Estate
Royal Mills
Esher
Surrey KT10 8BL
Tel: 0137 2465655
*Performance showers, shower
head and taps.*

The Water Monopoly
16–18 Lonsdale Road
London NW6 6RD
Tel: 020 7624 2636
*Antique and restored bathroom
furniture, fixtures and fittings.*

ARCHITECTURAL SALVAGE

Architectural Reclaim
Theobald's Park Road
Enfield EN2 9BG
Tel 020 8367 7577
*Flooring, baths, radiators and
windows.*

Lassco
St Michael's Church
Mark Street
London EC2A 4ER
Tel: 020 7749 9944
*Reclaimed baths, sinks,
fireplaces and stairs.*

Walcot Reclamation
108 Walcot Street
Bath BA1 5BG
Tel: 01225 44404
*Flooring, fireplaces, doors and
stone-work.*

*Italic numbers refer to the
illustrations.*

A

Aalto, Alvar, 19
accent lighting, 146
African furniture, *16*, *30*
ambient lighting, 146
ancient, definition, 17–19
Ando, Tadao, 19
apartments, Paris, 118–22,
  118–23, *152–5*, *153–4*
appliances, kitchens, 85
architects, 42
architectural details, 20, 60
  living areas, 81
  mirrors and, 142
architectural salvage, 27, 46,
  118–22, 150
architraves, 60
armchairs, 108
Art Deco, 23, 153
art objects, 134
artist's studio, Edwardian, 66–9,
  66–9
assessing space, 41
Avoine, Pierre d', *22–3*
Azman Owens, 46

B

balance, 13
Ball, Jonathan, 46
balustrades, 60
Barcelona chair, 14
barn conversions, 23, *42*
Barragan, Luis, 19
basements, 42, 72
bathing areas, *92–3*, 93
  fixtures and fittings, 150
  lighting, *149*
  mirrors, 142, *142*
bedrooms, *88–91*, 89–90
beds, *88–91*, 90
Bell, Nikki, 41, 70–2, *145*,
  148
benches, 111
Bertoia, Harry, 81, *123*, 154
blinds, 138
brick factory, New Jersey, 62–4,
  62–5
building regulations, 42, 58

C

carpets, 56, 141
ceiling roses, 60

chairs:
  mixing old and new, 107
  practical chairs, *110–13*, 111
chandeliers, 148
china:
  displaying, 134
  functional ceramics, 30
church conversions, 55, 58
clothes, storage, 90, 116
Coates, Nigel, 50
Cocteau, Jean, 154
coexistence, 13
collections, 131
  displaying, 132–4, *132–7*
Colombo, Elena, *6*
colour:
  connections, 26
  juxtaposition, 24
  unifying spaces, 49
  upholstery fabrics, 108
Comme des Garçons, 14
computers, 94
concrete floors, 56, 57, *57*
connections, 24, 26–7
Conran, Sir Terence, 66
conservation laws, 42
contexts, 14
cookers, 85
cooking areas, *82–5*, *83–5*
cottages, Georgian, 66–9,
  66–9
coving, 60
cupboards, 116, 150
curtains, 138, *140–1*, 141
cushions, 138, 141
cutlery, *19*, *30*, *31*

D

de Vries, Barbara, 26–7, 41,
  62–4
Delsalle, J.F., *44*, 124–7
desks, 94, *94–5*
dimmer switches, 148
dining areas, *84–7*, 85
  furniture, *110–13*, 111
displays, 132–4, *132–7*
Dixon, Tom, *149*
domestic architecture:
  fusion of old and new, 46
  radical alterations, 45
  relaxing areas, 78
  structural alterations, 42
  structure, 38–41
doors and doorways, 50, *52*
door handles, 150

E

Eames, Charles, 19, *111*, *120*,
  121, 127
Eames, Ray, *121*, 127
eating areas, *84–7*, 85
  furniture, *110–13*, 111
Edwardian artist's studio, 66–9,
  66–9
Edwardian house, 124–7, *124–7*
electricity sockets, 146
engineers, 42
extensions:
  fusion of old and new, *22–3*,
    23, 46
  roof extensions, 42

F

fabrics, 138–41, *138–41*
  upholstery, 108
Feng, Han, 23, 131
Fernlund and Logan, 42, 45
Findlay, Ushida, 28
fire regulations, 42, 58
fireplaces, 60, *60–1*
fixtures and fittings, 150, *150–1*
  making connections, 27
floors, 56–7, *56–7*
  radical alterations, 45
  structural alterations, 50
focal points:
  mirrors, 142
  relaxing areas, 78
fridges, 85
furniture:
  African, *16*, *30*
  armchairs, 108
  chairs, *110–13*, 111
  eating areas, 85
  making connections, 26–7
  mixing old and new, 107
  occasional tables, *114–15*, 115
  practical tables, 111, *111–13*
  relaxing areas, 78, 108, *108–9*
  Shaker, 14
  sofas, 108
  stools, *114–15*, 115
  storage, 116, *116–17*
  working areas, 94

G

galleries, 45
Georgian houses:
  cottages, 66–9, *66–9*
  town houses, 70–2, *70–3*
  woodwork, 54

glass:
  floors, 57
  glassware, 28, 134, *137*
  mirror glass, 142
  windows, 54
Gordon, Alastair, 26–7, 41, 62–4
Gray, Eileen, 19
Gustafson, Max, 26

H

Habitat, 14, 19
handles, 150
Hawkinson, Laurie, 62
Herzog, Jacques, 14
home offices, 94, *94–5*
Horne, Pip, 23

I

IKEA, 14
industrial conversions:
  fusion of old and new, 46
  New Jersey brick factory,
    62–4, *62–5*
  radical alterations, 45
  relaxing areas, 78
  structural alterations, 42
  structure, 41
information lighting, 146
insulation, floors, 57

J

Jacobsen, Arne, *12*, 19, 24, *25*,
  113
Japan, 14
Jouve, Georges, 102, *103*
juxtapositions, 24–6

K

Kapoor, Anish, 23
Kawakubo, Rei, 14
kilims, 141
Kita, Toshiyuki, 127
kitchens, *82–5*, 83–5
  chairs, 111
  displays, 134
  fixtures and fittings, 150, *150–1*
  storage, 116
Knoll, 102, *102*, *108*, *111*

L

lamps, 148
Lander, Hugh, 46
Langlands, Ben, 41, 70–2, *145*,
  148

lanterns, paper, *149*
Le Corbusier, 19, 76, 130
Leitersdorf, Jonathan, 148
light:
  bathing areas, 93
  bedrooms, 90
  changing structures, 42
  lighting, 146–8, *146–9*
  mirrors, 142
  windows, 54
  working areas, 94, *94*
listed buildings, 42
living rooms, 78–81, *78–81*
loft conversions, 13, 23, 41
  architectural features, 60
  case study, 96–8, *96–9*
London, 13
  Edwardian artist's studio,
    66–9, *66–9*
  Georgian town houses, 70–2,
    70–3
Lot/ek, 46
Louvre, Paris, 14

M

machine age, 19
Mackintosh, Charles Rennie, 66
materials:
  bathing areas, 93
  floors, 56–7, *56–7*
  fusion of old and new, 46
  kitchens, 84
  making connections, 27
  textiles, 138–41, *138–41*
mats, tatami, *57*, 98
matting, 141
Mechiche, Frederic, *12*, 26, *43*,
  118–22
Mellor, David, 14
Meuron, Pierre de, 14
mezzanines, 45, 64
Mies van der Rohe, Ludwig, 14,
  19
minimalism, 19
  New York town house, 100–3,
    101–2
mirrors, 142, *142–3*
Miyake, Issey, 14
modern, definition, 19
Modernist Movement, 19
Morris, William, 106
Mortada, Andrew, 115

N

Naylor, Fiona, 42
New Jersey brick factory, 62–4,
  62–5

New York, 13
  loft conversions, 23
  town house, *100–3*, 101–2
Newson, Marc, 17

O

objects, displaying, 132–4,
  132–7
occasional tables, *114–15*, 115
office furniture, 116
offices, 94, *94–5*
open-plan areas:
  loft apartments, 96–8, *96–9*
  relaxing areas, 81

P

paint:
  floors, *56*
  stairs, 58
panelling, *53*, 60
paper lanterns, *149*
Paris, 13
  apartments, 118–22, *118–23*,
    152–5, 153–4
Pawson, John, 19, 23, 45
Pei, Ieoh Ming, 14
Perriand, Charlotte, 19, 102
pictures, 144, *144–5*
planning regulations, 42, 54, 60
plumbing, 93, 150
plywood flooring, *16*
Pop Art, 26
power sockets, 146
privacy:
  bathing areas, 93
  working areas, 94
Prouvé, Jean, *17*, 19, *108*

R

radiators, 150, *151*
radical alterations, 45
Randall, Nik, 45
recycling materials, 27, 46,
  118–22, 150
relaxing areas, 78–81, *78–81*
  furniture, 108, *108–9*
  occasional tables, *114–15*,
    115
Roberts, Stephen, 101
Rogers, Richard, 45
roof extensions, 42
room dividers, 81
rugs, 138, 141

S

Saatchi, Doris, 36, 76
screens:
  bathing areas, 93
  shoji screens, 28, *52*, *74–5*,
    93, 98, *99*
sculpture, 134
Shakers:
  colours, 26
  furniture, 14
shapes, 28
  juxtaposition, 24
  shelving, 150
shoji screens, 28, *52*, *74–5*, *93*,
  98, *99*
Shore, Ann, 49
showers, 93
skylights, 54, *54*, *66–7*, 69, *72*
slate floors, *14*
sleeping areas, 88–91, 89–90
Smith-Miller, Henry, 62
sofas, 108
space:
  assessing, 41
  extensions, 42
Spira, Rupert, *18*, 26–27, *53*,
  115, 132, *144*
Sporre, Yvonne, 148
spotlights, *149*
stairs, 58, *58–9*
standard lamps, 148
Starck, Philippe, 115
Stickland Coombe, 66–9
stone floors, *56*, 57
stools, *30*, *114–15*, 115
storage, 116, *116–17*
  clothes, 90, 116
  fixtures and fittings, 150
  kitchens, 84–5, 116
  relaxing areas, 81
structure:
  assessing space, 41
  changing, 42–5
  domestic architecture, 38–41
  fusion of old and new, 46
  low-key changes, 49
  radical alterations, 45
  walls and doors, 50
studio, Edwardian, 66–9, *66–9*
surveyors, 42

T

table lamps, 148
tables:
  eating areas, 85
  mixing old and new, 107

occasional tables, *114–15*, 115
practical tables, 111, *111–13*
work-tables, 14
taps, 150, *151*
task lighting, 146, 148
tatami mats, *57*, 98
Tate Modern, London, 14, *15*
technology, 19, 81
templates, 28
textiles, 138–41, *138–41*
  upholstery, 108
texture, contrasts, 24
Thonet, 154
throws, 138, 141
tiling, bathrooms, 93
town houses:
  Georgian, 70–2, *70–3*
  New York, *100–3*, 101–2

U

upholstery, 108
Ushida Findlay, 96–8
utilities:
  bathrooms, 93
  structural alterations, 50

V

van de Keuken, Gert, 23, 111,
  130, 132
Vasa, *103*, *132*
Victorian houses, 13
  bay windows, 54

W

walls:
  exposing surfaces, 50, *53*
  movable, 50, *52*
  structural alterations, 50
wardrobes, 116
Warhol, Andy, 26
white schemes, 26, 49
windows, 54
  skylights, 54, *54*, *66–7*, 69, *72*
wood:
  floors, 57, *57*
  shelving, 150
Woodgate, Terence, 108
work surfaces, kitchens, 84, 85
working areas, 94, *94–5*
Wright, Frank Lloyd, 19

Y

Yamamoto, Yohji, 14

Acknowledgements

Thank you Simon Upton for the wonderful photographs in this book and for your determination to keep to the point and to look for – and celebrate – ancient and modern at every opportunity. Thank you Lawrence Morton for a great design; the way you have used the photographs shows that you like them too!

Thank you Jacqui Small for commissioning me to work on this project. I am very pleased we worked together. Thank you Stuart Cooper for your vital commitment and input.

My biggest thanks to everyone who let us photograph their home – it was a privilege and a delight – and to everyone we met, for your kindness and support. The homes in this book are a mix. Some are the result of people making a space on their own, some are the result of people working with architects and designers, and some are the homes of architects and designers. Thank you Michael Benevento, Elena Colombo, Richard Ferretti and James Gager, Wendy and Fabian Friedland, Andrea Gentl and Marty Hyers, Alastair Gordon and Barbara de Vries, Gert van de Keuken, Ben Langlands and Nikki Bell, Jonathan Leitersdorf, Frederic Mechiche, Sir Giles and Lady Montagu-Pollock, Rupert and Caroline Spira, Yvonne Sporre, Simon Upton, Alannah Weston, and Greville and Sophie Worthington.